THE EVERYTHING®
GUIDE TO A HAPPY MARRIAGE

Dear Reader,

It is often said that therapists become therapists to heal themselves. While this is certainly the case for me, it's also true that I do this work because I love the intrigue and complexities of human behavior and relationships. I feel privileged when a couple opens up in therapy with me as their chosen guide. I'm honored to be trusted with their innermost secrets. To confide in a complete stranger with the hurt and tender aspects of your soul takes real courage and perhaps a little desperation. However, it is in those moments of desperate vulnerability that real healing takes place. And it's in those tender moments that I feel so emotionally connected to these two brave people.

For the past twenty-eight years I have been a witness to many marriages and been permitted to offer new concepts and approaches to assist them as they heal their wounded marriages and families. In my Making Marriage Work Workshops, I've seen couples open up and learn from other couples, sharing the most intimate trials and successes of their marriages—to help each other rise to the next level of what's possible in their relationships. My clients have taught me everything I understand about marriage. Through this book, Victoria Costello and I hope that you, too, will receive the benefit of their positive intentions and hard work as you strive to make your marriage work.

Sincerely,

Stephen Martin

THE

EVERYTHING
Series

These handy, accessible books give you all you need to tackle a difficult project, gain a new hobby, or even brush up on something you learned back in school but have since forgotten. You can choose to read from cover to cover or just pick out information from our four useful boxes.

 Alerts: Urgent warnings

 Essentials: Quick handy tips

 Facts: Important snippets of information

 Questions: Answers to common questions

When you're done reading, you can finally
say you know **EVERYTHING**®!

PUBLISHER Karen Cooper

DIRECTOR OF ACQUISITIONS AND INNOVATION Paula Munier

MANAGING EDITOR, EVERYTHING SERIES Lisa Laing

COPY CHIEF Casey Ebert

ACQUISITIONS EDITOR Katie McDonough

SENIOR DEVELOPMENT EDITOR Brett Palana-Shanahan

EDITORIAL ASSISTANT Hillary Thompson

Visit the entire Everything® series at *www.everything.com*

THE
EVERYTHING®
GUIDE TO
A HAPPY
MARRIAGE

Expert advice and information
for a happy life together

Stephen Martin, MFT, and Victoria Costello

Avon, Massachusetts

An Everything® Series Book.
Everything® and everything.com® are registered
trademarks of F+W Media, Inc.

Published by Adams Media, a division of F+W Media, Inc.
57 Littlefield Street, Avon, MA 02322 U.S.A.
www.adamsmedia.com

ISBN 10: 1-60550-134-4
ISBN 13: 978-1-60550-134-5

Printed in the United States of America.

J I H G F E D C B A

Library of Congress Cataloging-in-Publication Data
is available from the publisher.

This publication is designed to provide accurate and authoritative information with regard to the subject matter covered. It is sold with the understanding that the publisher is not engaged in rendering legal, accounting, or other
professional advice. If legal advice or other expert assistance is required, the
services of a competent professional person should be sought.
—From a *Declaration of Principles* jointly adopted by a Committee of the
American Bar Association and a Committee of Publishers and Associations

Many of the designations used by manufacturers and sellers to distinguish
their products are claimed as trademarks. Where those designations appear
in this book and Adams Media was aware of a trademark claim, the designations have been printed with initial capital letters.

This book is available at quantity discounts for bulk purchases.
For information, please call 1-800-289-0963.

This book is dedicated to the thousands of courageous couples I have seen over the past twenty-eight years in private marriage and family therapy sessions and in couples' workshops. I congratulate you all for persevering through the hard work of personal growth to reach mature marital love.

Acknowledgments

I wish to acknowledge my coauthor Victoria Costello who has listened to me talk ceaselessly about this work. With extraordinary sensitivity, she took my thoughts and gave birth to them in this book. Without her creative talent and perseverance, it would not exist.

Contents

Top Ten Things You Can Do to Make Your Marriage Work

1. Marry your best friend
2. Hibernate during the first year of marriage to cement your relationship
3. Agree on joint financial goals, review these regularly
4. Take each other out on dates
5. Have a weekly check-in to discuss your issues (all marriages have issues)
6. Keep your fights private
7. Get marital therapy before you get to the point where you hate each other
8. Have children only when you believe you'll stay together for the next eighteen years to raise them
9. Divorce only as a last resort
10. Celebrate your marriage every day!

Introduction

WHAT IS LOVE? LOVE is everything. At the same time, it's not enough. How can both statements be true? In too many marriages, there are fleeting feelings of romance posing for love. If this book does nothing else, it should demonstrate the difference. For any marriage to work, love must be understood and experienced as a thoughtful commitment to an imperfect person.

In a good marriage, the excitement of romantic love ultimately leads to a lively, ongoing communication, a deep knowing of your partner's most intimate joys and fears, sacred sex, a bedrock of trust, and a set of practical agreements to guide how you'll conduct your lives together. When all these things are present you have fulfilled the promise of love in marriage. For the majority of happy couples, this process takes many years together to achieve—and the results of these long-term marriages are well worth the effort. In the chapters that follow, the knowledge and skills required to sustain the love that brought you together are laid out with step-by-step guides for traversing the areas that throw roadblocks into every marriage. These areas of contention are self, money, sex, and children, and because these topics wreak the most havoc in marriage, they receive the most attention.

Other chapters address the special challenges that frequently occur in new marriages and stepfamilies. The joys of long-term marriages are also explored. Finally, Stephen Martin offers his sober assessment of what anyone should consider before making the decision to go through with a divorce.

To help you find out where your marriage is weak and where it's strong, be sure to try the Marriage Self-Test in Appendix A; in fact, it may be the perfect place to start reading. This test works best if you and your partner answer the questions separately, and discuss the results together, but there are insights available to anyone who opens up to the process. The same can be said for the rest of this book, and of marriage itself. One of you can have a positive impact on the marriage by identifying and changing your own thoughts and behaviors, but if both of you take on the same tasks, a working marriage is virtually guaranteed.

Chapter 1

What Makes Marriage Work?

FROM THE MOMENT Romeo sets his eyes on Juliet to the fairy-tale climax when Cinderella captures her prince, young people are taught that falling in love is the one and only essential requirement for marriage. Unfortunately, many carry this fantasy through multiple failed marriages. While love is absolutely necessary in a marital relationship, if you wish to make your marriage work over the long haul then the love between you can't simply be based on feelings. That's because feelings change like moods. If romance were the sole factor determining the duration of a union, most marriages would end in six months. Love must be both a feeling and a decision if it's to be the basis for a working marriage.

Marriage Is Like a Three-Legged Race

As a child you may have had picnics where you competed in three-legged races. Two players had their middle legs tied together, so that between the two of you, you had three legs, with the objective of running in unison. This game requires great dexterity. Runners must bring their shared middle leg forward in a stride and rhythm that is comfortable for both. It is not an easy task, but eventually the pair learns how to run together by coordinating two bodies as one. Marriage requires a similar mind and skill set.

The secret to running as a three-legged team is harmony and collaboration. Telling your partner he's doing everything wrong only slows you both down. The left leg (you) feels it is superior to the right leg (him). Since you are joined together in this race, criticizing him harshly is actually attacking and sabotaging yourself.

If you lose the race and berate your partner for his performance you are guaranteeing your team will fail the next race as well. In a three-legged race you either win together or you lose together. This is also true in marriage. Either you both succeed, or you both fail. Blaming your partner for a marriage failure is like the left leg criticizing the right leg. It may briefly make the left leg feel better, but it will not remedy what's not working in your team.

 Question

How is a good marriage different from a bad one?
If marriage is viewed as a competitive sport, a good marriage is a cooperative effort that produces a winning team. A bad marriage is where the two players put more efforts into their individual successes, and thus create a losing team.

One of the biggest and most consequential errors a couple makes is to assume teamwork skills come naturally. They don't. The most negative consequence of this mistaken view is a failure to identify and learn the necessary skills required to make marriage work. Marriage is no different than learning how to drive a car or play a team sport like baseball. Finishing with the three-legged race analogy, to have a chance of winning the two of you must operate as one. This requires practice and patience as you learn how to support each other through the trial and error of learning how to move, step by step, through your combined lives.

The Illusion of True Love as Effortless

Can you imagine climbing Mt. Everest without any training, preparation, or forethought? Picture it: All you have to guide you up the highest mountain in the world is the conceptual idea that getting to the top would be very rewarding. Then off you go, with enthusiasm and the romantic notion of adding this achievement to your resume. It is not an exaggeration to say that many people of all ages and educational levels get married with about the same amount of forethought and preparation as the would-be climbers in this silly example. What they soon discover is that succeeding in a successful long-term marriage (not a so-called bad marriage) is as challenging as climbing Mt. Everest.

 Fact

Since the Middle Ages, Western culture has made romantic love the primary source of life's meaning, wholeness, and ecstasy. Paradoxically, the experience of falling in and out of romantic love is also the source of the deepest wound in the Western psyche.

More than Luck

To get another myth out of the way, it takes much more than luck or good karma to produce harmony and happiness within marriage. Obviously luck or karma may play a part, and there are some couples that fit together so well they prompt others to wonder if they've not been blessed as soul mates, meaning a couple who are destined for each other. Maybe, but this lucky couple still needs to decide who's going to take out the garbage and who'll do laundry. However destined, they're not saints and they'll have to cope with each other's flaws. Even the luckiest couples face the same reality: Marriage is a challenge that requires new skills, practice, and enormous patience.

If any area of marriage requires luck, one would have to say it's the mate selection process. Those who marry young have to look for the right life partner without really understanding what marriage entails, and without knowing the important ways in which both may change ten, twenty, or thirty years down the road. Then there are all the unknowable ups and downs life will deliver that will test you as a couple and a family.

Essential

Marital love is a rational commitment made between two imperfect humans who believe that within marriage they can support each other to be better people than they would be alone.

CHOOSING THE RIGHT MATE

Certainly some individuals have more self knowledge at an earlier age, giving them a better set of criteria to work with in choosing someone compatible, while others will have to learn by painful trial and error about who the appropriate partner for them may be, picking the wrong person first, perhaps experiencing a "broken heart" or a painful divorce. Then again, if experience were the main factor, it would follow that second and third marriages should exhibit higher success rates than firsts—and, unfortunately, this just isn't true.

What the data suggest is that young or old, and whether it's your first, second, or third marriage, men and women are marrying without having learned important lessons about who they are, what they need from a partner, and the essential skills required in any marriage. This sad reality makes a persuasive case for premarital counseling, practice with couple communication, and financial management— whatever the two can do to prepare for the rigors of marriage.

THE MUST HAVES

Clinical observation of successful marriages indicates that good relationships have three essential components that qualify them as superior: trust, honesty, and effective communication. To these, for the purposes of making this *Everything® Guide* useful for most relationships and each stage of marriage, please add teamwork, conscious daily practice, and humor to this "must-do list." Simply put, if most or all of these qualities exist in your marriage the chance of achieving success as partners is greatly enhanced.

Practice and Teamwork

All team sports require that the individual players give up their personal egos for the benefit of the team. For example, on a football team, it is imperative for a quarterback to be blocked by his front line in order to advance the ball. Every successful quarterback congratulates his front line when they win, often giving his front line the primary credit for any yards gained. When they lose he's very discrete about criticizing his players and does so only in private. Successful football teams work together as a group. As with all team sports, they succeed or fail together.

 Question

What is success in marriage?
When both partners report that the relationship is challenging but also very rewarding. Each knows he's a better person due to the personal growth he achieves through his marriage. He's also gratified knowing his partner has also grown as a person.

As illustrated by the three-legged race analogy, marriage is a team sport. Teamwork and practice at working as a team are essential to marital success. The team cooperates, coordinates, and collaborates. Every day provides another opportunity for the successfully married couple to practice its dexterity as a team. In other words, you will never be done practicing these essential relationship skills. There's always more to learn from each other. That's one of the great joys of a long-term committed relationship. It's also one of its challenges.

Honor Each Victory as Your Own

You and your spouse will find that if your marriage is happy, there are times when just one of you is in the spotlight, akin to making the big play in football. Perhaps she's made a big sale at the office, or he's completed a new patio in the backyard. The smart couple realizes that each partner's individual achievement would not be possible without the active support of the other. This is no more true in marriages where both partners work outside the home than in those where one is a stay-at-home parent; it pertains to all marriages. When you became a team, you signed on to be the best you could be, and also to do all you could to help your partner realize fulfillment. This means you treat each other's successes as your own. This is the essence of teamwork.

 Fact

In a self-oriented culture, it's often counterintuitive for couples to hear that—for the benefit of the marriage—each person must place the needs of his partner at the same level of importance as his own. But this is the essence of mature, marital love. Kindness and generosity are contagious. What you give is what you receive in return.

Recognize and Celebrate Each Success

Another important part of marriage and all forms of teamwork is celebrating your victories together, both the smaller and larger ones. A small success may be getting dinner on the table by 6 P.M. instead of 7 P.M. A larger success may be meeting your savings goal for the year. Happy marriages balance the needs of the individuals without sacrificing the harmony of the couple. Achieving this end may be as complicated as balancing on parallel bars, or running a three-legged race. Married life was never intended to be easy.

Communication

In a healthy marriage you have chosen to be "in love" with your best friend, which is really another way of saying that marriage requires going beyond being struck by Cupid's arrow, the single act used to symbolize how—in myth, movies, and literature—love magically begins "at first sight." The promise of romance is to find blissful union with your beloved. In order for spouses to get close to this lovely goal, each needs qualities more closely associated with platonic love, the generous relating seen in close friendships where one friend puts the well-being of the other above his own desire to possess another. It also means telling your partner the whole truth and staying in close communication—just as you would do with your best friend.

The reason why real love becomes more challenging after the first six months of a relationship is because at this point you can no longer coast on the initial high of romantic attraction, the period when overlooking flaws is easy. After these thrilling emotions subside, you and your partner must really begin to communicate about some of the harder issues that have arisen between you. These must include your most intimate thoughts and feelings. And if your marital partner is your best friend, you can and will want to share all of yourself with him—the good, the bad, and the ugly.

> When Sandy and Tim first met and dated, she was immediately drawn to the way he carefully considered questions and problems put to him before giving an answer or opinion. "I could see him thinking. He never took the easy way out," she said. Well, after seven years of marriage, Sandy's admiration for her husband's deliberateness had turned into impatience and boredom. What or who had changed? With two jobs and two kids, a mortgage, and other money pressures,

Tim and Sandy had lost their desire and commitment to listen and learn more about each other, to get below the surface of things. Those were the nice "frills" of relationship, niceties they'd abandoned to coping with the stress and practical demands of daily life. The solution to their communication breakdown was to turn this order of priorities on its head; set aside time, and, if need be involve a therapist, to help them learn ways to communicate on a deeper, more meaningful level. Sandy had to honestly tell Tim that his manner of speaking had a way of creating a wall between them in conversations. Tim had to share his frustrations about not being heard. In that way, each was able to get more of the potential support the other had to offer, and move them forward from this stuck place in their relationship.

If you cannot share important information with your partner you have a serious problem, and you need to do some hard soul searching to find a way to remedy this situation. A successful marital relationship has a good communication style as the primary predictor of its success. The communication is effective, immediate, and results oriented, meaning it modifies behavior when that's necessary for the harmony of the marriage. How do you get to this level of communication with your spouse? Chapter 4 addresses this question in depth.

Keep It Private

Too often, one partner in a couple tells friends outside the marriage information about intimate aspects of her marital life before she shares this information with her partner. This unhealthy dynamic exists because trust, honesty, and complete truthfulness have not been established inside the marriage. The problem usually goes back to judgments made between partners, allowing defensiveness and fear to enter and hamper the communication process.

When people are intimate, it is essential that judgments be openly acknowledged and correctly managed so that judgmental communication does not destroy the harmony within the marriage.

With judgment comes disapproval and anger, hurt, and defensive-ness, all the negative qualities that can deaden intimacy. What can you do if you are not currently honest, trusting, and open with your partner? You must first ask yourself is this is an appropriate relation-ship for you. If it is appropriate, then you must learn and practice effective communication skills with your partner. If it's not, then deal with the issue of appropriateness.

Essential

What is left unspoken will not go away; it will fester and begin to eat at the foundations of your relationship. To keep the chan-nels of communication open, set aside thirty minutes as a weekly "check-in time" with your partner.

Assuming your answer is that this is an appropriate relation-ship, and this means there are shared values, respect, and love for each other present in your marriage, but you are still feeling judged by your partner, the two of you need to begin the process of talking about these issues. Honest communication is essential for success. Without truthfulness, how can trust be established? With-out trust, how can love survive? Without love, how can intimacy continue? Several techniques for positive communication between spouses are presented in Chapter 4, when the subject is treated in depth.

Trust

True love is experienced in a long-term relationship as both love and hate. That's because people are extremely complicated beings, and in marriage a person often projects his internal feelings upon his partner. For example, if a woman is feeling unappreciated in her marriage, she may fantasize about how much better it might be with someone new. Instead of owning her frustrations and desires, she may then project these feelings onto her husband, and accuse him of going elsewhere for intimate companionship when nothing of the kind has taken place. Projection is a normal dynamic in close relationships. The goal in marriage is not to eradicate projections. Rather it is to recognize them for what they are: your feelings put on another. Once you own your feelings as yours, not his, you can sort out what's really going on. Remember, it's a natural, necessary process to do this sorting-out on a regular basis.

For as long as the two of you remain married, you are each other's lover, principal companion, sounding board, coparent, and householder. That's an enormous amount to have invested in another human being. This doesn't mean you don't have to maintain a healthy boundary between the two of you. You do, and this ability requires equal parts self-knowledge and active communication between partners. It's also important to understand that you can't satisfy all of your partner's needs. For that matter, it's usually better for this not to be the case, that is, to be a couple in a wider community of family and friends. Trust in marriage comes from the belief that each of you is there to stay and are equally committed to working on those issues that are hurting the relationship.

 **Alert**

The secret of long-term marriage is not to be in total agreement on all things, at all times. Rather, in a happy marriage you agree on which things it's okay to disagree on, and you commit to finding a workable compromise on the most important relationship issues where there are substantial differences. For most couples, these are finances, sexuality, and children.

Commitment Has Many Sides

If two people stay married long enough they realize that long-term marriage challenges them in ways they would never have considered. As the old story goes, when a famous person was once asked if he had ever considered divorce, he replied, "Divorce no, murder yes." So, you may wonder, how can anyone possibly hold onto his trust for a spouse in such perilous terrain?

Commitment is what keeps you in the game, especially when your temporarily hurt or angry feelings may shout, "You're in grave danger, get out!"

Being in love brings wonderful physical sensations and feelings, but mature love is not a feeling that comes and goes. Mature love does not define itself by a temporary emotion. Love is more permanent, and that is why marital love must be a commitment based on a rational decision two people make before they marry. Without this solid commitment, most marriages will not last one year. Commitment is the essential foundation of marital trust.

Honesty

Honesty is your ability to tell the truth day after day. Not just when it's easy, but also when it's hard. Honesty is a deep emotional and spiritual commitment to examine your feelings and your motives and be totally truthful with yourself and your partner. Honesty is perhaps the most important quality associated with character and integrity. The opposite of honesty is dishonesty. Dishonesty is manipulation— manipulation of yourself and of others. Many people justify their dishonesty on the grounds that the truth will hurt other people's feelings. Once rationalized, dishonesty is transformed from phoniness into nobility, and the result is a superficial relationship.

> Since Janice considered her recent month-long affair with Stewart "just a fling," she decided she would not tell Jonathan that it had ever taken place. But it weighed on her. Whenever Jonathan did or said something nice, such as complementing her appearance or a meal, the guilt she felt was unbearable, prompting her to withdraw and not express appreciation in return. Finally, Jonathan figured out what had happened by

way of Janice's credit card bills, the tangible proof to add to his growing suspicions, which had been based solely on her "strange behavior." Janice and Jonathan came to marriage therapy at this point. In addition to the affair, the most important issue for this couple was the honesty missing from their communication not just about the affair, but in many other areas where they closed each other out. In order to put more honesty in their interactions, Janice and Jonathan had to work hard on trust.

Personal dishonesty is hiding the truth from your own conscious awareness. However, the body never lies, and when you are dishonest within yourself, your body will eventually manifest sickness and disease as a compensation for the disharmony. When you have no access to your real self, you are an open target for disaster. Until you are able to understand yourself and become truly honest, you cannot share deeply with your partner. And when you are being manipulated in a relationship, it feels like you have been sold a bill of goods.

Essential

Being honest with your mate is not the same as telling him every negative thought that pops into your head. Neither should it be about blaming him. Instead of lashing out with, "You didn't do the dishes tonight because you don't care about me," you can say, "I feel stressed out and unsupported when you don't keep your agreement to do the dishes." When you express a real feeling, there's a much better chance of getting to conflict resolution.

Honesty must first begin within you, and then it spreads to your relationships. As a result, only the honest have satisfying relationships. In healthy relationships partners find kind and sensitive ways to tell the truth. Knowing that the truth shall set you free, both parties patiently and loving unfold their truth before their partner. Not in a cruel or harsh way, but in a gentle, caring, thoughtful manner. With the unfolding of truth, the relationship grows into all that it is possible for it to become. You face the tough issues. You address the difficult places. Then, as the truth unfolds, the relationship grows into a loving bond with which you can always handle the truth. With honesty, relationships can transform from superficial and unsatisfying to supportive and mutually fulfilling. With honesty, relationships grow into their highest potential. With dishonesty, relationships shrink and then die.

Humor

One of the more reliable signs that a marriage is working is if the two partners laugh together, frequently. It's well known that laughter has a health benefit, as Norman Cousins wrote about based on personal experience in his groundbreaking book *Anatomy of an Illness*. He was given a death sentence by doctors and decided to laugh his way back to health. His book is about how that worked for him.

Laughter is a very rational way to accept the totally irrational aspects of life, including the tough times in a marriage. Expecting two people to agree all the time is the most irrational expectation you can have. People are prone to asking unanswerable questions and taking life far too seriously. Humor is a way of making everything ridiculous and in so doing we accept the unacceptable.

Laurie and Robb have been looking forward to taking their first vacation without their two young children for over a year. With her mother committed to babysitting, time off from Robb's job secured, and a week selected, the only unresolved part is where they'd go. He wants to lie on a tropical beach and play golf. She wants to do an ambitious walking tour in an exotic place. The discussion has remained civil until now, when Robb, feeling unappreciated for the hours he puts in at work, blows up and accuses Laurie of being selfish and unconcerned about his needs. Instead of going tit for tat and throwing an accusation back at him, Laurie chuckles and pauses. Then she looks Robb in the eye and says, "How about we go to Maui. I whip you in a round of golf on day one, and you climb Mount Kiluea with me on day two." The use of humor (Laurie doesn't play golf) and the suggestion of compromise immediately changed the temperature between them and allowed them to arrive at a mutually agreeable resolution.

So laughter in relationships can break up the "stuckness" in the same way a lubricant frees up a rusty axle. Laughter allows you to relax and enjoy each other even though you may disagree.

So how do you accept the unacceptable? Humor is often the easiest way. It allows you to put things in prospective and let go of rigidity. After the tensions are loosened you can see more clearly and be in harmony again instead of disharmony. Humor is a major component of all successful long-term relationships.

A Plan B (When Everything Goes Wrong)

Natural disasters are a fact of life. Each time a flood, hurricane, or earthquake strikes, lessons are learned about improving readiness for each type of disaster the next time. The foundations of buildings are reinforced, levies are built taller, and evacuation plans are improved.

Like hurricanes and earthquakes, marital disasters can be predicted and mitigated if steps are taken to ease the problems before they become too serious.

Marriage counselors know the typical problems that occur in marriage, and thoughtful couples can tend to their relationships before they are thrown into disaster clean-up mode. Unfortunately, most people seek help with their marriage after the levy has broken. Of course, cleaning up after the disaster has occurred is much harder than changing and preparing before the disaster strikes. Yet human nature is such that very few couples prepare ahead for potential problems.

Where the Levies Break in a Marriage

There are four major areas that have the potential to weaken most marital relationships. Preparing for these potential problems is like reinforcing the levees that broke in New Orleans. The four areas where problems are likely to occur and where growth is possible are:

- **Self and Boundaries:** Maintaining your individual identity as you create an interdependent, not dependent, relationship with your spouse
- **Money:** Creating a productive financial partnership with your spouse, not using money as an instrument of power but as a foundation for mutual fulfillment
- **Sex:** Restoring a fulfilling, respectful sexual union, not making sex a bargaining chip in a marital power game but as the basis for an emotional and spiritual connection for your relationship, and a foundation for self-growth.
- **Family:** Building safety, nurturance, and boundaries for your children; living in community with your extended family, friends, and neighbors.

This does not mean every relationship shall experience these problems. They are the areas of potential problems and definite areas to place your attention if you wish to strengthen your marriage.

Every couple should know in detail the potential sticky issues in their relationship and should have a disaster preparedness plan waiting in case these issues become overwhelming and destructive. Every marriage is only as strong as the weakest link, and knowing where the weak links are will strengthen and support your marriage so that when difficulties arise, you have a plan of action.

How to Assess Your Marriage

When real estate values fluctuate, people keep a close eye on how much their house is worth, what needs repairing, and what maintenance chores are currently required. Homeowners are diligent about

keeping their home valuable, because for most people a home constitutes their life savings. So, just as you know the net worth of your
most prized material possession, your home, it follows that you must
also calculate the value and status of the most important nonmaterial thing: your marriage as the cornerstone of your family. It's time
to figure out what in your marriage needs replacing and what can be
addressed simply through improved maintenance.

To draw an analogy between real estate and marriage may seem
odd, but if you and your partner were like most couples you'd agree
that your marriage and family is of far more value than your home.
Homes can be replaced, while divorce can produce total financial
and emotional devastation. Only you and your partner can assess
the value of your marriage.

In the Marriage Self-Test that is sampled here and provided in
full in Appendix A, you can get a fair evaluation of the current value
of your marriage.

For example, consider these four self-test questions:

- On a scale of one to ten, how satisfied are you in your
  marriage?
- On a scale of one to ten, how satisfied is your partner in
  your marriage?
- Are you optimistic about the future of your marriage?
- Is your partner optimistic about the future of the marriage?

In each case you are asked to first answer the question from
your own point of view. And then, consider the same question as if
answering for your partner. This exercise is often very revealing for
couples, especially if they sit down and compare and discuss their
answers. If you really wish to assess the value of your marriage, the
ten questions that make up this Marriage Self-Test should begin a
lively debate between you and your partner. One thing is certain:
Good marriages are not an accident. Bad marriages, like bad real
estate, tend to be neglected.

Chapter 2

Danger Signs in a Marriage

YOU'VE HEARD THE bad news: The odds of having a successful marriage are in the neighborhood of 50 percent. For second marriages, the odds worsen to 35 percent. Yet the vast majority of people marry, and if a first marriage fails, both partners are likely to remarry—proof that the majority of adults today desperately want to make marriage work. Statistics also show the average marriage lasts 6.8 years. Probably, both parties in these marriages noticed problems early on in the relationship that they unfortunately either didn't recognize as danger signs, or they simply didn't know what to do about them—and didn't ask.

Don't Give Up Too Soon

Marriage therapists are much more likely to see a couple after the marriage reaches the breaking point, rather than early in the process of breaking down. Both partners at this distressing juncture will often be experiencing despair, and they'll ask the therapist's opinion about whether they should "just end it." The real feelings lurking behind such a question actually sound more like this, "We're so tired of trying the same old things and getting nowhere in our relationship. Can't you give us something new to try?" The answer is yes, if you're willing to work hard at it, and learn the signs of marital trouble.

 Fact

Divorce remains at historic highs compared with the 1950s. According to the U.S. Census, one-half of the first marriages of baby boomer couples will end in divorce or separation. About ⅔ of divorced women and ¾ of these divorced men eventually remarry, although divorce rates in remarriage are higher than those in first marriages.

Both men and women experience marital disaffection or the dying-out of love between two spouses. The process is painful for everyone; sometimes as agonizing for one or both partners as the death of a loved one. What's also true is that many married men and women come to the conclusion that their marriage is over prematurely. That is, they give up from exhaustion and despair when there are still things that can be done to save the marriage.

The Blame Game

When a relationship begins to turn sour, inevitably people blame their partner. Being right and making the other wrong starts to hold more value to each spouse than the goal of maintaining love, peace, and harmony in the relationship. Underlying whatever the couple is arguing about, be it housekeeping, an affair, or one partner's long hours at the office, there are deep unacknowledged hurts and disappointments. A woman often feels unappreciated or unloved. A man feels nagged or neglected. These are two major themes heard in marriage therapy. The skilled therapist knows these are often symptoms of other underlying problems. The danger is that the couple never goes below the surface of the antagonisms reigning in the present, never knows what they're actually fighting about, and each blames the other for the standoff that results.

In this scenario of battling spouses, the ego reigns supreme and love begins to die. When harsh words, physical distance, and immature behaviors such as irrational spending have replaced the gestures of love, it's sometimes difficult to understand what's actually going on in your marriage. It appears to have fallen completely apart and you can't recall why you ever "fell in love" with this person in the first place.

 Question

What is the most frequent reason given for the failure of a marriage?
The vast majority of divorced men and women surveyed by divorce mediators Lynn Gigy, PhD, and Joan B. Kelly of the Northern California Mediation Center say an unmet emotional need (such as "growing apart") ended their marriages. Two other frequent problems given are a high-conflict (or demeaning) relationship, and one partner's attempts to control the other. Only a quarter blame an extramarital affair.

Falling out of love is often given as the reason when a breakdown occurs within the first five years of a marriage. This is true especially when the couple's original process of falling in love did not include the development of a solid friendship. If you're at this stage, your fight-or-flight instinct is telling you to get out as fast as you can. However, if you have a bond of friendship with your spouse and take the time to learn more about human behavior and why most people take counterproductive actions when stress occurs in intimate relationships, there is hope. You not only stand a fair chance of halting the destruction of your marriage, but you can also take a huge step forward in divorce-proofing it for the long haul. Each of the major potential danger signs is deconstructed in this chapter so you might better see how and why a negative dynamic has entered your relationship, and begin to do something about it. Understanding must precede action.

When Talking Stops

The destructive action that precedes the breakdown of good communication in a marriage is not simply a refusal to speak or share feelings; it's an excess of criticisms being volleyed back and forth between you and your partner. When you articulate your differences or make a complaint, it's the tendency to condemn each other, to make one way wrong and the other right, rather than pinpointing the real issue or celebrating the variety between you. Before you can ever hope to do the latter, you must learn how to deal with the inevitable grievances you'll have about each other in a manner that solves the issue, at least arrives at a compromise, but doesn't blame or make the person wrong.

An illuminating study was done on the attribution of blame in marriage. This study looked into who tends to do the blaming, whom or what they blame for marital tensions, and what this means in a marriage. If, for example, John is being inconsiderate to Sharon by speaking rudely to her (more than once over a period of a week) she has two possible targets for her blame, one external and the other internal. An external cause for John's negative behavior would be: "he's overly stressed at work." An internal cause would include: "he's an uncaring person." If Sharon chooses the internal cause for John's rudeness, she's more likely to respond in kind; that is, by speaking rudely or nastily back to him. If, however, she chooses to believe his rudeness stems from a high stress level, she's more likely to respond with kindness.

He Really Can't Read Your Mind

One of the most common mistakes individuals make in their marital communication is expecting a partner to understand what they need and want without telling them. This is a big mistake. Once the expectation is set, and your partner doesn't fulfill these wants, anger can result. "If you truly loved me, you would know what I want." How? Why would you believe this to be true? Yet many couples operate with this kind of assumption.

The way out of this mistake is to take the risk of being rejected and express exactly what you want and need. Becoming vulnerable is essential for couples to communicate effectively. Without taking the risk of being honest and forthright, you can create the possibility of a breakdown in your communication system. Over years, such a breakdown can destroy a relationship.

 Question

What is excess criticism in a marriage?
Excess criticism is when your conversation contains more negative than positive aspects, either in tone, body language, or actual words spoken. It's when you look at your spouse with fear instead of love, and when you look for the differences between the two of you, rather than searching for similarities and common interests.

Sex Interrupted

Within a marriage no other aspect of your lives together is as sacred as your sexual expression. If sexual relations diminish or disappear in a marriage, without an understanding and mutual agreement among the spouses, this is a major danger sign for the marriage.

However, sexuality as a dimension of marriage can never be isolated from other aspects of the relationship, especially mutual respect and communication.

The Latin root of the word "intimate" is *intus*, which means *within*. To let your partner into the most private parts within your being—those thoughts, deepest feelings, and erotic desires you share with no one else—requires trust, gentle communication, and time. When problems show up in this area, the solution must also take in many parts of the relationship. Again, because of its unique power to restore you individually and as a couple, dealing with sexual danger signs must be a high priority.

Sexual Healing

Within your sexual relationship there is emotional healing to be found for both of you. Healthy sexual expression heals, restores, and energizes. The healing comes when the two of you permit each other to become the most vulnerable and emotionally expressive that each can be. Loving sexual expression is the place where you come together in joy, pleasure, gratitude, humor, and dancing bodies. The smart couple does not allow this sacred space to be assaulted. The partners in a healthy marriage protect this place above all because of its power and healing quality. Sexuality is the glue that holds the couple together when you would prefer to just walk away. Once sexuality is disturbed, emotional healing must occur if the marriage is to continue in an intimate manner.

Essential

Frequent sex brings health and happiness. There are now studies galore to prove what most people know by personal experience. Several studies have shown that sex once or twice a week improves heart functioning and stress tolerance, and boosts immunity. Recently, researchers detailed how orgasms increase levels of the hormone oxytocin, the so-called love hormone, which helps us bond and build trust. Higher oxytocin has also been linked with a feeling of generosity.

Frequency Matters

After asking thousands of couples in his marriage therapy practice of twenty-five years how often each partner would prefer to have sex if the other would go along with that wish, Stephen Martin reports the vast majority of men say once a day or more while most women say once a week or less. This large difference in male and female levels of sexual desire may not be the case in your marriage, but it is a frequent enough dynamic to be aware of its potential as a sign of marital trouble particularly at times of high stress, for instance, after the birth of a baby or when overtime is required of one of you at work. If the frequency of your sex has become an area of contention, the frustration and potential alienation that results for both partners can sow seeds of major trouble now or later in the marriage. Chapters 8 and 9 offer problems and solutions for this common area of marital breakdown.

Emotional Drama

The cause of your anger in an intimate relationship is rarely what you think it is—initially. Quite often, lurking beneath the anger that occurs between spouses is an unacknowledged feeling that is unconscious to the one who's expressing her anger. This is why it is necessary to look past anger to find the unseen feeling you or your partner (if he is the angry one) needs to resolve. Anger is more often fear or sadness, insecurity, or despair in disguise. Expressing anger for most men is socially safe because our culture views anger as strong, while sadness is seen as weak. For men and women, getting in touch with your anger is far more important than expressing it. Once you understand why you are angry, you can handle the real issue and not strike out at the nearest target.

Your Feelings, Your Responsibility

The problem most people have with an internal disturbance is that they blame someone else for their agitated feelings. No one but you can be responsible for the feelings you are having. It is seductive to blame others, because then you do not have to take responsibility in the matter. However once you hold others accountable for your feelings, you can only quiet those internal feelings if the other person changes. It is much smarter to recognize that all your feelings are your own responsibility, and then work to create inner peace from that context.

When you find yourself in a relationship feeling fear and anger, you need to find the causes of those feelings, and the pathway out of these self-defeating attitudes. Otherwise they will destroy you and the relationship you are hoping to build. Fear has many causes, but usually it is the result of attempting to control life so you will not re-experience a past event that produced the fear you fear to feel again.

 Fact

Women "flood." Men "stonewall." Based on his laboratory research with married couples, psychologist John Gottman, PhD, reports that 70 percent of the time a marital conflict begins with a woman raising a complaint to the attention of the man. When the woman overloads the man with complaints, Gottman calls this "flooding." He says that 80 percent of the time, the man in this situation is not talking, or he's in some other way resisting or sabotaging discussion of his partner's complaint.

THE PAST HAUNTS THE PRESENT

Perhaps you have experienced a horrific event in the past and are bringing the feelings of that occurrence into the present. By carrying the unhealthy experience within, you are probably hoping to stop feeling what you felt when that experience occurred before. Thus you are unconsciously holding onto emotional junk as a defense against feeling it again. Better to let it go and trust that if it shows up again you shall know how to handle this one differently. Then you can really face your fears with a new power and with new vitality.

Carrying old hurts and pain around inside is disastrous for you, your partner, and everyone who is close to you. An appropriate path away from fear is to surrender to what you cannot change, and accept the mystery of life and the gift that is beyond human understanding. But before most find this secret pathway out of fear, they get bogged down in the futile attempt to control life, other people, their lover, and even their own unchangeable nature, which will lead to frustration and more fear.

FINDING STRENGTH IN LOVE

Your greatest strengths and those of your partner are also your greatest weaknesses. You first fall in love with what you experience as the strengths in your partner, and then you experience the shadow side of these same qualities. For example, strong-willed people are first viewed as clear-minded and determined, but eventually this strength reveals its dark side as your awareness grows. The strength is then seen as stubbornness and inflexibility. Every coin has two sides. In truth you need both sides, for only with contrast can anything exist. Good is good because bad is bad. Beauty is beauty because ugly is ugly. Paradox demands tension between opposites. Handling the paradox is the key to contentment. How well you manage the tension determines the health of your relationship.

E ssential

If you have to choose between friendship or the love relationship you have with a married partner, always put your friendship first. Platonic love, the kind shared by friends, requires that you think about the other person's needs, not just about your own or what you think you want from the marriage.

Spending Out of Balance

One of the most contentious issues that couples fight about is money. When individuals have different values about how money should be spent, or when one of you is a spender and the other a saver, the resulting tensions can be formidable. There is much more detail about solving common marital money problems in Chapters 6 and 7. For now, you should be aware of the fact that there are times in a marriage when excessive or sudden spending is not about money at all. This is when a money problem is actually disguising another, sometimes larger problem in a marriage, akin to a temperature or cough preceding a serious bout of the flu. It's important to pay attention to early symptoms of any malady.

More Time Apart than Together

How much time to spend together versus time apart is one of the most important issues for a married couple to resolve. There is no right answer. There's only what works for you and your partner. That said, when what had been a comfortable balance of time spent apart and together suddenly changes without discussion or agreement between the partners, you have a marital danger sign. Many factors come into play and must be considered. Among these factors are high stress, extreme parenting or caretaker demands, the tone of your emotional relationship, and the level of trust you have for each other.

 **Alert**

There are inherently bad times to talk about difficult issues. For example, don't bring up a touchy topic when you and your partner are rushed or under stress. Never criticize him in front of another person—no matter who it is.

A Man and His Cave

Men (as a generality), and some women, because of the way they operate emotionally, need more time alone to ponder a problem or personal disappointment. This is sometimes referred to as a man needing to go into his cave to nurse a wound or replenish his emotional reserves. And while there may not be a cave in your backyard, you may find your husband spending untold hours working on his car or in the shop. He's found a modern-day cave for his manly retreat. It's important for a spouse to allow a man time to do this psychic replenishing. However, if it goes on too long (an amount of time that will vary by the person and situation) there's the danger that the couple may lose a meaningful emotional connection. This is always a balancing act, and frankly, women tend to err on the side of too much interference as opposed to giving a man space when he needs to spend time alone "in his cave."

Meanwhile, many a woman (and some men) prefers to jointly address and process things by talking about what concerns her. A woman may do this with female friends, but if her husband is generally unable or unwilling to listen to her problems, she may emotionally withdraw from him. That is another marital danger sign.

Mood Swings

If your marriage is in frequent turmoil you have another indication that the union is in danger of coming apart. What's not as easy to see is why this may be happening; why some days your time together is joyous, and why on many other days you're at each other's throats. "We are as sick as our secrets" psychologist Carl Jung famously stated. Until it erupts, most couples do not see the approaching danger signs of serious emotional conflict, because they don't spend enough time learning about the inner self, and its unconscious motivations.

One of the places to look for clues to what is happening below the surface is the often-long list of expectations each of you brought into marriage and whether those expectations are reasonable. Women, now that you've seen the way he spends many an evening sitting mutely in front of the TV and leaves the bathroom a disaster area after bathing, do you fear he is no longer the romantic, attentive prince you married? Men, now that she nags you regularly about not doing household chores you'd agreed were in your column but not done, is she no longer the adoring goddess you fell in love with? These may sound like exaggerations, but unfortunately they accurately describe the sort of let down that many newly married men and women experience and the disparity between the expectations and reality of marriage for those who haven't looked closely at the differences between romance and love. What do unrealistic expectations have to do with those subterranean feelings that are now sabotaging your marriage?

Donna is a thirty-three-year-old, married, stay-at-home mother to Jodie, a two-year-old handful. Per their marital agreement, Donna's husband Christopher works long hours so that Donna has the ability to stay home with Jodie. They also agreed on a plan to have a second child before Donna returns to her career as a nurse. The problem for this couple is that their time spent with each other has been reduced to the two extremes of bickering or silence. Donna is frustrated and misses having adult conversations. She feels Christopher could try harder to listen and support her.

Christopher is often exhausted at the end of the day and feels nagged and unappreciated when Donna complains about the poor quality of their conversation. To him it sounds like a demand. While all these issues are real and would benefit from improved communication between Donna and Christopher, there is a deeper problem. Donna grew up as an only child of divorced parents. One of her unspoken and partly unconscious reasons for marriage was so that "she'd never feel lonely again."

Before Donna and Christopher can do the kind of straightforward problem solving that would help alleviate their end-of-day tensions—perhaps set a specific time each week when a babysitter is secured—Donna needs to own her deeper feelings and share them with her husband. Not only will this act of self disclosure help her clear her old hurt, it will draw the two of them together in a deeper emotional bond based on Christopher's intimate knowledge of his wife's dreams and fears.

Both men and women are susceptible to disappointment when the initial romance of marriage wears thin, or when their original expectations fail to materialize. Both sexes express marital disaffection similarly—by blaming the other partner and withdrawing emotionally from the relationship. These patterns are what create the violent mood swings in a dying relationship just when the opposite behaviors are needed to save it. As previously discussed, these positive behaviors include being honest with each other, increasing the level and quality of your communication, negotiating your differences, and not taking your partner's words and actions personally.

Chapter 3

Power Sharing in Marriage

HISTORICALLY, COUPLES FACING irreconcilable marital strains stayed together because they had to, whether for social, legal, or economic reasons. Today, there is little social disapproval attached to divorce. For the first time in (Western) history, legal marriage is based on something other than property or social convention, and for most marriages, that other thing is emotional support. However, because all this change has come about so quickly, today's husbands and wives must individually come to terms with how to allocate power, privilege, and responsibility. The old rules are gone and with new mores in flux, power sharing is an area that trips up many couples.

Reinventing History: This Is Not Your Parents' Marriage

The social and economic changes reshaping the institution of marriage have entered American society gradually but steadily since the mid-1970s. That means a great many of those marrying in the last two decades grew up in households where male and female roles were undergoing a rocky transition. Many experienced divorce as children, with no models of a successful marriage between equals to draw on for their own adult lives.

With today's *new normal* of equal marriage translating into multiple breadwinners paying the bills, and divvying up housework and childcare on an ad hoc basis, there's a great deal of confusion out there about how to handle it all. How long should a new mother (or father) stay home with a newborn child? How much "help" with household or parenting should be expected of the spouse who works outside the home? Who makes sure the bills are paid on time? Who decorates the house? How are buying decisions made? For better or worse, there are no fixed answers to any of these questions. So, if you're feeling overwhelmed and unsure of how to share power in your marriage, first take a breath—you're not alone.

Second, it's important to honor the emotional support you give each other no matter how well or not so well power sharing is going in your marriage. Know that power sharing will be a process of negotiation that will last as long as your marriage.

Your emotional support is the foundation for the discussions and negotiations that will be necessary in order to reach agreement about how to share power as you structure your day-to-day lives together. When you have this unbreakable emotional bond, each of you knows that no matter how difficult your disagreements may be, both of you are committed to seeing the process through.

 Question

What is emotional support?
It is the love bond (a commitment) that exists between two people who want to join their separateness into one. It is the ability to communicate feelings. It is the quality of deep friendship that must exist in a marriage if it is to survive the challenges facing every couple.

No Operating Instructions

Where do you look for models of equal power sharing in marriage? No other formal relationship in our lives operates with this ideal of equality. Between parents and children, parents have the legal and moral authority and responsibility. In most workplaces, there is an established form of authority. One person is the boss, accountable to people superior to him; if he is the CEO, he's accountable to a board of directors. Marriage, however, is not a business contract. If it were, the relationship would be reduced to exchanging services with fines paid for breaking the agreement.

America's original marriage laws were based on English common law and later legal statutes, which only gave men legal standing. With this legal standing came the right to control all marital property, including his wife's wages and inheritance, with or without her consent. He even had the right to control her body and the children.

It took nearly two thousand years for Western culture to grant women equal rights in property and marriage (England began changing its laws in the 1850s; by 1900, the United States had followed suit). While fundamentalist religions may continue to uphold a traditional patriarchal view of marriage, these communities are still subject to modern society's laws and customs.

Beware the "Old Rules"

While this history of marriage may seem archaic, even irrelevant to today's couples, what is often not well understood is how vestiges of these cultural traditions can leak into modern minds, or at least the unconscious parts of those minds, muddying the waters for couples attempting to split up rights and responsibilities equally in a marriage.

The man who stays home with the kids while his wife works—whether this joint decision came about voluntarily or because of a lost job—may find he has to fight feelings of shame over not being a "proper" provider for his family. Or the woman who juggles kids and a job and feels inadequate in each role must fight her unconscious belief that she should be strictly a mother and wife and not forge an independent work life.

In today's equal marriages, spouses share the belief that they will make their own joint agreements about power sharing, including all decisions affecting money, sex, property, and children. However, they're given little guidance on how to go about it, and can find themselves battling outmoded beliefs they may not even realize affect them. Do not make the mistake of underestimating the complexity involved in this process, or the need for flexibility as conditions in your marriage change over time.

 **Alert**

What you don't believe can still hurt you. Outmoded beliefs—for instance, the notion that a man who stays home to care for children while his wife works is being unmanly—can undermine your relationship and disrupt the agreements you've made with each other, especially during stressful times.

Examples of unforeseen life changes that can bring major consequences for marital agreements are when one of you loses a job and opts to return to college for retraining, or when a child or elderly family member needs intensive caretaking. Your operating agreements will require creativity, diligence, and regular monitoring. The process of reaching and maintaining them will test the depths and strength of your emotional bond. Frankly, if power sharing were easy, there would not be a 50 percent divorce rate.

Defining Your Ideal Marriage

You probably know a couple where the husband either works at home or is the stay-at-home parent while the wife goes to work elsewhere five days a week. You may know more than one couple where the woman earns more than her spouse. You may be a new mother who is on paid or unpaid maternity leave from a demanding job and plan to go back in a set period of time. All of these options are now common but would have been unheard of or simply unusual even forty years ago. That doesn't make them any easier to sort out for many modern couples, but sort them out you must.

Priority Issues for Marital Power-Sharing Negotiations

- Housework and lawn care if you have one.
- Budgeting: Saving, investing, and spending. Even just dealing with communal expenses, there's the challenge of defining and differentiating necessities and frills. Food, of course, is a basic need, but what about eating out? Cable TV, probably, but what about the football season package from your satellite TV service?
- Will you have an equal right to spend? What if one partner earns a disproportionate amount of the family income? In other words, what is joint and what is individual money?
- Will you have children? How many? Plus, there are all the related decisions about who stays home, if anyone, childcare, private versus public school, and many, many more.
- Sex: How often? What kind? Is your relationship sexually monogamous? If not, is your ground rule don't ask and don't tell? Or is it tell all?
- How much time is it okay to spend alone or with other friends and activities outside the marriage?

Each of these areas is dealt with in more depth in one or more subsequent chapters. The questions are raised here to highlight the many issues, which, unlike most other relationships in your life, must be addressed and resolved satisfactorily for another person with equal say over most of the decisions that affect you both. When people marry later in life, with developed careers and children from former marriages, things get even more complex. However, all of these issues are solvable ones. It's often a good idea to involve one or more third parties to help you. Depending on the area in question you may visit a marriage therapist, minister, lawyer, or accountant to take advantage of their knowledge of tried and true solutions to common issues.

Different Kinds of Power: His, Hers, and Ours

Many couples divide up the tasks of marriage, including household chores, the kids, and the finances into two columns: his and hers. Within these two separate domains, usually there is an agreement about what decisions should be made communally and which ones the individual "in charge" of a particular area can make alone. That way, the decision making is divided according to negotiated task assignments.

 Fact

Having a husband creates on average an extra seven hours a week of housework for women, according to a University of Michigan 2005 study of a nationally representative sample of U.S. families. For men, the picture is very different: A wife saves a man from having to do an hour more of housework each week.

This works until one of the partners disapproves of a decision or feels left out of the process. Then renegotiation occurs. It is during the negotiation stage that most couples have problems. For example, a couple begins with the following agreement: Every Saturday morning a grocery list is posted on the refrigerator to which they both contribute; then on Sunday afternoon, she does the food shopping. During the week, he cooks two nights, she cooks three, each is on his own one night, and they eat out together on the other. The days for each are selected and maintained on at least a monthly basis.

There are, however, easily spotted pitfalls in such agreements; for example, on the very likely occasion when she works late and dinner is not made.

- Does he make it for the two of them?
- Does she pick up his next cooking night?

- Is this decided ahead of time or left to spontaneous decision making?
- What if the shopping doesn't get done, one orders takeout, the other picks around at the dregs of the refrigerator, and both end up feeling deprived and let down?

Now you may feel this is awfully petty material for a marital dispute, and it's true. However, any marriage therapist will tell you that his office hours are filled with even more trivial arguments that, if left to fester, can and do slowly erode a marriage.

If this couple does not know how to communicate needs, complaints, or limits, then they will begin to develop negative feelings about each other. Hurt, anger, and distrust show up, and most couples do not understand how to navigate these difficult feelings and begin to emotionally distance themselves from each other. As the tension increases, the hurts multiply, and soon you find yourself in a major emotional disaster. Then love turns to anger and distrust, and soon the relationship seems irreparable.

Creating a Working Partnership

The way to create an effective working partnership is by combining clear, regular communication and skilled negotiation. You must learn how to communicate and negotiate your wants, needs, and desires, and be willing to accept your partner's needs as equally legitimate. This form of communication is very sophisticated but essential. To get to a place where you can make agreements that are reliable, thus less likely to break down and cause emotional distress, each partner must come to terms with where his strengths and weakness lie. Which one of you is more detail oriented and thus better with money? Whose job permits working at home in order to stay with a sick child? These questions require soul-searching honesty as well as practical assessments by each partner of what she is going to deliver—not what she hopes she might be able to do on a good day.

With this type of communication you can you come up with a suitable agreement to handle your practical needs as a couple. Life will never flow seamlessly; it throws wrenches into the best-laid plans. That's why agreements have back-up plans and ways to communicate feelings when things go wrong. If only one of you wants to repair your broken communication, the process will stall. It is necessary that both partners learn how to deal with the difficult issues in the relationship and not sweep messes under the carpet.

 **Alert**

Learning the skill of mind reading is not the right goal for marriage! It's not your job to detect what's bothering your partner from studying his body language or the length of his silences. Instead, learn how and when to ask questions so he can tell you what he's thinking and feeling. Too many spouses put too much stock in their ability to read a partner's mind.

Many issues in the course of the week can be let go, but if you find yourself angry and distrusting toward your partner, you will need to spend time repairing this difficulty. Without effort, work, and diligence, the relationship will become emotionally distant, dissatisfying, and empty.

So as you approach the issue of power sharing, be advised that you will probably need to take a step back on a regular basis to see why and how your agreements may be breaking down. Then, address the quality and quantity of communication you're using to repair those broken agreements. To be proactive and guard against this unsatisfactory outcome, the two of you can recognize and systematically address all the areas of responsibility and decision making that you face as a couple, as well as your respective strengths and weaknesses, in order to come up with a plan that is likely to work. Tools to assist you in this process follow.

Sharing Housework: Make a Contract

The division of labor in housekeeping is one of those areas of nego-tiation that should be among the easiest of all marital problems to solve but rarely is. One reason why is that a man traditionally has not done his "fair share" of cleaning, food shopping, cooking, wash-ing clothes, and dishwashing. It may be that his mother trained him poorly, not putting these traditionally female duties on his boyhood list of chores. He may not "believe" that housework is "women's work," but his behavior is saying otherwise. Another exacerbating problem is that when a man doesn't pick up after himself, a woman often makes the mistake of personalizing his action into a negative statement about her; that he doesn't appreciate or love her, for exam-ple. Even for younger men old habits die hard, but that doesn't let him off the hook.

 Fact

Women whose husbands do housework feel more open to sexual activity, researchers say. Ladies, you may wish to leave this page of the book open for your husband to come upon "accidentally." Or just give him the information straight as part of your negotia-tions around housework. The reason given by researchers for this phenomenon is that a woman whose chores checklist is complete goes to bed more relaxed and open to her mate. It makes sense.

Sometimes a man will swear that he does not notice the dis-crepancy in who does how much housework. Then he apologizes and changes his behavior—for a short period of time—putting the woman in the position of the "nag," a role no woman wants to play. To rectify this observation and performance gap, a good technique is to prepare a thorough contract in which you list the essential chores in and relating to household management.

In this contract, make two columns after each chore. One will record who does the task presently. A second column will reflect the product of your negotiation: who agrees to take on that task in the future. Among the likely tasks besides food shopping, cooking, laundry, cleaning the bathrooms, vacuuming carpets, and dusting don't forget to list childcare assignments, checkbook balancing, mailing or paying bills online, dealing with health insurance paperwork, and all the other essential life-management tasks.

 Question

How much housework is done by the average married male compare to a married female?

Things are getting more equal but they're not there yet. The amount of housework done by men has increased, according to the University of Michigan's Institute for Social Research (ISR). In 1976, women did an average of twenty-six hours of housework a week, compared with about seventeen hours in 2005. Men did about six hours of housework a week in 1976, compared with about thirteen hours in 2005.

The benefit of doing your housework negotiation as both a chart and a contract is that it forces you both to acknowledge what the current reality is and what you agree you want it to be. Although it may feel like an elementary school exercise at first, it's important to embrace this process until housekeeping is a smooth operation most of the time in your household.

The Weekly Check-In

A good habit for couples to get into is to have scheduled meetings when they present practical and emotional issues that need to be aired and discussed. Just as a well-functioning business has regular meetings to make certain all the employees work as a team, a good relationship practices the same procedure. For some reason, too many couples don't see the necessity of such meetings at home, while they easily accept this practice as a given at work. Perhaps they are hopeful that what is not discussed will just go away. However, as it is in business, so it goes (or doesn't) in a relationship.

 **Alert**

What is left unspoken will not go away. It will fester and begin to eat at the foundations of your relationship.

First you need to schedule a regular check-in conversation. Once or twice a month works well, but if you find yourself in disharmony, perhaps once a week is necessary. Once the time is scheduled, it must be viewed as private time where your focus and attention is fully present with no distractions permitted, meaning that children are occupied or attended to and cell phones are off.

Within this period for communication, each of you can state feelings or ask questions while the other listens and then answers. Questions can include:

- What have you not communicated that you want to talk about?
- What haven't you been acknowledged for that you want me to have recognized?
- What's not working? What's working better?

You can put your questions in many forms, but ultimately the point of these discussions is to get out the feelings that are bottled up and destroying the free flow of love and respect.

The length of time for a regular check-in should probably be forty-five to sixty minutes, no less. Most couples can handle this communication by themselves; however, if the tension is too intense, and the communication breaks down into rage and anger, an outside mediator may be needed. Good communication is essential for healthy relationships. Regularly scheduled check-ins will keep a relationship healthy and alive. It is important that honesty and trust exist for the process to work. Without these basics, the process can break down and the relationship will fester until eventually it dies. Vibrant couples regularly communicate about the agreements they've made to each other.

Chapter 4

He Said, She Said

WHEN MARRIED COUPLES are asked to name their biggest problem, most say it is poor communication. Good communication skills pull a couple together, while poor skills push the two apart. Of course, communication between any two people can be challenging. The reason why it's harder between spouses has as much to do with nature as nurture; meaning differences between the sexes that are both biological and cultural in origin. It's these differences that complicate matters and explain (in part) why·the thing that should get simpler over time—communication between a man and a woman who spend the greater part of their days and nights together—needs to be constantly relearned, practiced, and refined for the marriage to stay strong.

Why Communication Is Important

Good communication is the lifeline that holds the two of you together and allows all the other important things in married life—sexuality, parenting, financial planning, and community—to flourish. Communication means sharing verbally and nonverbally so that a message is accepted and understood by your partner. Contrary to what many people think, the goal of communication in marriage is not always to produce agreement. In fact, many marriages go on for decades without the partners agreeing on important issues like childrearing styles or financial priorities.

When differences between partners are large and concern vital areas of life, the two partners must negotiate until they reach a compromise between their two diverging points of view. To get to such a compromise, step one is always effective communication, which always involves blame-free talking and active listening. To be effective, active listening requires genuine interest in what your partner is saying. It also requires you to make verbal responses demonstrating that you understand his point of view.

All communication can be broken down into three components: content, tone, and body language (nonverbal cues). Many people assume that content is the largest component of communication since they view most conversation as an exchange of information. You may be surprised to learn that only 7 percent of communication is content, while 38 percent is tone, and a full 55 percent is body language, those nonverbal cues (facial expression, arms crossed or not, shoulders raised or relaxed) by the one delivering the message. These latter two items, tone and nonverbal messages, also tend to be influenced by gender differences.

 Question

What is active listening?
It's when you take in what your partner has to say with empathy and compassion. You aim to fully understand him. You don't make judgments about the content of what he says. Because you're not making a judgment, you don't need to agree with what he says. This is a time to make listening to him your only agenda. You are his friend, not a judge.

The Ways Women and Men Communicate

Although not uniformly present in all couples, gender differences in communication style and content preferences are common enough to wreak havoc in many marriages. It's important to remember that

these differences can make communication in marriage more difficult, but on their own they do not cause marital breakdowns.

The Way Women Communicate

Research is now proving beyond a shadow of a doubt what
you've probably known since you entered adolescence and began
paying serious attention to the opposite sex: Men and women tend to
talk for different reasons, and the two sexes process information differently. Scientists have discovered that women really do hear *more*
than men. Just think about the running debates that go on between
spouses about the preferred volume of a TV or stereo. Then apply
this principle to the tone used by a man and a woman in an argument. Which spouse is more likely to be impacted by a raised voice?

 Fact

According to noted marriage researcher John Gottman, PhD,
women are the ones who most often bring up difficult topics for
discussion with their spouses, in fact 80 percent of the time. Gottman, author of *The Seven Principles for Making Marriage Work*,
notes that this communication dynamic is dominant in the "good"
as well as the "bad" marriages he observes in controlled laboratory settings.

Neurologists also say that men see and perceive visual stimuli
more clearly than women do. Think about maps and directions as
an example. Then apply this principle to your facial expression during a difficult discussion with your husband. What is more likely
to create distance: a calm, sympathetic expression or a scowl? An
easier example might be how difficult it is for most men to *not* ogle a
shapely female who happens to be walking by.

The implications of biological and neurological differences
between men and women in marriage are manifold. Women are
more verbally oriented, while men operate and make decisions

based more on what they see. In the realm of couple communication, women are more prone to talk things out, while men typically mull things over—alone.

Women talk as a way of connecting and to relieve anxiety. A woman also prefers to think out loud, without necessarily looking for an immediate solution to a problem. Because women are more inclined to communicate when they are upset, a woman's silence often means more than the same behavior from a man. It may signal her alienation, particularly if previous attempts to be heard and understood by a partner have not been satisfying.

The Way Men Communicate

Men talk in order to exchange information, to solve problems, or, if they're with other men, to engage in friendly verbal competition. When anxious or angry, men will often seek solitude rather than talk, at least as an immediate response. Of course, each person is a unique combination of what is defined here. Your husband may be more of a talker than your girlfriend's more taciturn spouse. It's possible that you may be the more circumspect one in your marriage.

Essential

Avoiding piling on and conflating different issues when the two of you communicate. Topic A must be resolved before you move on to topic B. No substitutions are allowed until the first issue is settled. If need be, set up another time to discuss topic B.

From the fascinating observations of married couples done by John Gottman, PhD, in a laboratory setting it's been shown that women bring up most of the tricky issues for discussion in a marriage. The same research, which includes the monitoring of physical body changes, also shows that a man takes longer to recover from verbal conflict than his wife. What do all these data say about men and women in communication? Primarily, that on top of the possible personality differences that exist between any two people, a husband and wife must also take into account probable gender differences.

When Emotional Needs Differ

Different people have different emotional needs and preferred levels of intimacy in a marital relationship. These needs range from a measure of personal privacy within the relationship to a fairly constant state of emotional and physical connectedness between spouses. This can become a problem if you are married to someone who has very different needs from yours. For example, the person who wants to experience deep connectedness most evenings can become frustrated if her partner does not want to have as many deep conversations about the nature and meaning of their relationship.

Often, the one seeking more emotional intimacy will judge the partner who prefers less frequency and depth of contact as being shallow or less caring about the relationship. This creates tension within the relationship, leaving both partners unsatisfied. In marriage therapy, the one wanting emotional intimacy often complains that her partner does not love her, which is usually not accurate. What is true is that each has a preference for a different style of relating. Sometimes it comes down to one partner wanting always to communicate her feelings of appreciation and love in words, while the other prefers to do it through his actions. Both are expressing love; it is just done in different ways.

The choice of pronouns in this section is not a coincidence. Typically, the woman wants more emotional communication with words, while the man prefers fewer words. The male often prefers to express his feelings in sexual expression, while the female wants verbal interaction and heart connectedness first, and then sexual expression. However, it is not always the female who complains about a partner being emotionally distant. Many men have the same complaint about women. On balance though, the male usually prefers less emotional intimacy through conversation, and more emotional intimacy through sexuality.

The issue for couples already married and in a committed relationship is what to do when your emotional needs are different. The first step is to cease making the other wrong for his difference, and stop judging this difference between the two of you as evidence of dysfunction. Less verbal communication is not necessarily bad, unhealthy, or wrong; it is merely less verbal communication.

Timing Is Everything

Marital problems are like toothaches. If ignored, they only fester and becomes more painful. This makes communication about the problem absolutely necessary. However, complaints and sensitive topics raised with your partner at the wrong time or in the wrong place can worsen rather than help you deal with a touchy issue. Because of a woman's verbal advantages over a man, it's especially important for a wife to know when to bring up a potentially difficult topic for discussion with her husband—as well as how.

Even a question as simple to a woman as "How was your day?" if asked as soon as the man walks in the door after a day of work, can feel like an unwelcome demand or even an attack. What's under attack from the man's point of view is his need for some period of recovery, relaxation, and freedom from all the demands that have been made on him in the course of that day.

While typically associated with men, this same dynamic can be reversed if you are a woman who comes home from a highly stressful job and feels the need for solitude before engaging with your spouse after a long day. Unfortunately, since most women who work outside the home also carry the brunt of childcare and household chores, the idea of a woman asking for a brief downtime at the end of her work day may not appear practical. This makes it all the more important for the two of you to deal with this as an issue for negotiation —but only when the time is right. So when should you bring up an issue with your partner? Try not to choose one of these moments.

- When rushed or stressed (morning rush, bedtime crush, while paying bills)
- During sex

- While discussing another difficult issue (one at a time)
- When one of you is depressed, drunk, or sick
- Right after getting home from work
- When you're with other people

The only way to establish your preferences about the timing of a potentially difficult topic is to communicate with each other about when and where to hold such a discussion. There is also a right way and a wrong way to verbalize your feelings about your partner's behavior.

- Do say, "I need to go sit alone in the den and watch the news before we talk."
- Don't say, "Leave me alone. You never give me any time to catch my breath."

The first is a statement about your needs. The second is an accusation and a blaming statement. Which would you rather hear?

Give Your Partner Warning

Sometimes a man or woman prefers to be given advance notice or warning about his partner's need for a time "to talk." Identifying the general topic and scheduling such talks for later that day or even later in the week can allow him to organize his thoughts ahead of time. Advance notice also enables him to identify potential emotional reactions to which he may be vulnerable and help him keep such emotions out of the conversation, making problem solving more likely. The same dynamic holds true when a topic is more sensitive for the woman. A man can ease the existing tension between them by giving her notice of his intention to address the issue of concern, giving her the chance to prepare if the time is off in the future.

Committing to a more in-depth weekly, biweekly, or monthly clearing process also enhances good communication. Clearing processes are scheduled appointments when couples agree to communicate about topics that they would rather not address. Very often, it is not what is said that creates tension; it is what is left unsaid. The unspoken arises within the relationship and slowly strangles the love and the bond between the two. Conflicts usually occur from what hasn't been said. It is important to keep communication open, free, and healthy; the clearing process will ensure that happens.

Essential

When you touch base at the end of a day, a brief exchange works best. It can help the one who's stressed get relief by airing a concern that is not about your relationship, be it an episode with a difficult boss or a child's teacher. The key is for the listener to validate his partner's emotions—but not to criticize or offer unsolicited advice. Being able to count on having someone who's on your side is one of the joys of a marriage that works.

How Best to Talk and Listen

A basic exercise Stephen Martin has labeled "Statement, Restatement, Agreement" (SRA) offers couples a good way to practice active listening. An SRA exercise begins with one of the parties, in this example a woman, making a clear and concise statement, while the other partner listens. Once the speaker has finished, the listener reports back what he thinks he's heard. If his restatement is not correct, the woman repeats her statement until the listener has clearly received her message. Then the listener finds some agreement within what is said. Perhaps the only thing he can agree with is how his partner feels. Perhaps he can agree with all that is expressed. The exercise is designed to build places of agreement so that the relationship can get back on course.

What you're doing is a process of statement and restatement until you reach an agreement. Here is an example of repeating back a partner's statement until you're sure of his meaning:

Statement: "Why didn't you let me know you were going to be late? I've been up for hours, listening for your car."

Restatement: "So you're really mad just because I got back late from the trip."

Statement: "No, that's not what I said. It's because you didn't call and tell me you were going to be late."

Restatement: "Okay, so it's not that I ran late, just that I didn't let you know."

Statement: "Right! Next time please just call. I was worried, and I wasn't sure what time you left."

Restatement: "Okay. Next time I'll call and give you a heads-up."

After the first partner has spoken, you change sides, and the other begins with a statement while the second partner listens, then reports back, and then finds some point of agreement.

In summary, to effectively do the basic SRA exercise, you both must:

- Take turns being the speaker and the listener
- Actively listen and understand
- Don't assume anything; ask
- Ask directly for what you want
- Make a request, not a demand
- Don't criticize or blame within your requests
- Carefully pick the time, place, and tone

Over time, you will discover how he best receives what you have to say, whether the two of you are presently in conflict or not. Does he prefer advance notice? Is a weekend morning the best time? Touch generally enhances his ability to listen. With this vital knowledge, you can adjust your choice of words, tone, and timing to best reach him. To do this, you must put yourself in your partner's shoes.

As you can see, this list of dos and don'ts for the SRA exercise can just as easily apply to all good couple communication.

The Problem with Anger

The hardest part of communication for men and women, but especially women, is delivering an angry statement or response. Anger is an emotion that is culturally defined as being more appropriate for men, and less so for women. As a result, many women have trouble expressing anger. Often a woman will repress her anger, internalize the feelings, and become depressed. A depressed person is also shut down and thus unavailable to her partner. This emotional state for either partner is harmful to marriage.

Too much expressed anger or repressed anger is bad for any relationship. As discussed in Chapter 5, "Ten Rules of Fair Fighting," it is the responsibility of the angry partner to vent his excess anger elsewhere rather than dump it on his spouse. It is also the responsibility of the one repressing anger to unearth her feelings and get "unstuck" by verbalizing what's bothering her. Good communicators learn how to create and develop grounds rules and abide by these ground rules whenever conflict and anger are present in their communication. For example, taking time outs when emotions get too hot is one useful ground rule.

"You" Messages Versus "I" Messages

Whenever speaking to your partner, and especially in times of conflict, always speak in "I" messages as opposed to "You" messages. "I" messages are statements about how "I feel," while "You" messages are statements about your partner, often accusative and judgmental in nature. If you want to tell your spouse something about his behavior that's bothering you without making him defensive, learn the difference between an "I" message and a "You" message.

Sharon is a stay-at-home mom. Her husband Tom works outside the home. At the end of the day, Sharon often feels Tom is unfairly critical of her, and then she responds defensively. For example, when Tom walks in the front door and sees toys and clothes in disarray on the floor, he'll say something like "Jeez, what a mess." In response, Sharon lashes out, saying: "I work hard all day with the kids, too." These tensions, and the stress and exhaustion behind them, are very common when one partner stays home to care for young children and the other works outside the home.

While she may not be able to make the tensions disappear, there's another, more effective way Sharon can express her complaint to Tom. She can say: "When you speak to me like that, I become hurt and angry, and then I can't listen to you."

With this delivery, Sharon owns her feeling and asks for what she needs.

A "You" message blames and inflames. An "I" message speaks to the issue at hand, and de-escalates an argument.

Pick Your Fights Carefully

Just as right timing, and the right choice of words are keys to solid couple communication, so too is your choice of topic. You may wonder, "Isn't a problem a problem if I think it is?" Quite simply, a secret of successful marriages is that each partner overlooks the majority of annoying things the other does—even if she finds the behavior irritating.

In any marriage where both partners have so much on the line, meaning your emotional support, financial stability, sexual identity, and even your standing in the community, you are extremely interdependent and vulnerable to each other. This reality should be acknowledged as a cause for celebration and caution. It's a celebration because you enjoy the privilege of living your life more fully in a loving, supportive partnership. However, you must exercise caution because any marriage can only handle so much conflict, and any spouse can only receive so much criticism before the person and the marriage wither and die.

 **Alert**

Don't sweat the small stuff. In a successful marriage relationship, one partner overlooks the vast majority of the other's irritating behaviors—without comment. In other words, she picks her battles wisely.

The warning to pick your battles wisely underscores the point that any two people can find an endless number of things to disagree on or criticize each other about. Diverging housekeeping styles, spending habits, definitions of staying in touch (for example, not calling when coming home late), insufficient sex or conversation—the list goes on and on as any married person knows. If you attack your partner on all these issues, you will without a doubt destroy your marriage.

Offensive Behaviors on a Scale of One to Ten

An old saying applies here: "Don't sweat the small stuff. And it's all small stuff." Although everything that causes marital conflict is obviously not "small stuff," if you put yourself through the exercise of ranking every complaint on a scale of importance from zero to ten, and then drop off your list of things to bring to your partner's attention anything below a nine, you'll get the meaning of this admonition. Examples of potentially irritating behaviors that would land at five or below on most readers' offensive behavior scales include:

- He repeats the same jokes or stories to you and others (everybody does it; get over it)
- She doesn't clean the kitchen as thoroughly as you do
- He wears paint-stained or beat up "comfortable" clothes around the house or to the supermarket

- She watches TV shows or reads books you find boring or lowbrow
- He burps or blows his nose too loudly when others are in the room

Offensive? Maybe. Deal breakers? Probably not. You may wish to write down your own list of your partner's offensive behaviors and then go ahead and give each a score of zero to ten. If his changing his behavior is truly essential to your well-being—that is, it affects your safety, security, respect, peace of mind, or minimum standards for civil intercourse—then yes, go ahead and raise it for discussion. Of course, your other option is to simply live with it, knowing that your partner has his own list of your faults, too. From these long lists, ideally, both of you will choose carefully.

 Fact

Asking for something always works better than demanding it. Even when you have every right to make a demand, why not use the more effective technique in order to get what you want?

Identifying Necessary Discussions

If you find yourself on either end of a constant stream of bickering with your partner, especially if you bicker about the same issue over and over, that is probably an area that requires careful discussion between the two of you. Before you begin that discussion, there are some important questions for each of you to consider.

- Is the issue at hand an essential one (it involves safety, security, respect, peace of mind, or a minimum standard of civil intercourse)?
- Is it a potentially solvable issue around which you are likely to reach mutual agreement if you put your minds to it?

- Is the conflict over a fundamental, unsolvable difference requiring a compromise that would be unlikely to fully satisfy either of you but which, if enacted, would make the marriage workable?

An example of a solvable issue is how soon after dinner to do the dishes. If this is an area of constant bickering, by all means, sit down and settle on an agreement, splitting the duty or exchanging it for another, like laundry or cooking.

An unsolvable but vital issue for discussion might be that he is Jewish, she is Catholic, and both would like to raise the kids in the religion of his or her upbringing. In this case, whatever compromise is arrived at will likely offer only partial satisfaction to both husband and wife. That doesn't mean it cannot be made to work. In both of these cases, discussion is necessary and will likely be productive.

 **Alert**

> Respond, don't react. Spouses are very good at "pushing each other's buttons." Then you wonder why your arguments never get anywhere. One key to effective marital communication is to resist going back to the old sore points; instead stop and speak from your heart using an "I" message.

Spotting Emotional Baggage

There's another sort of necessary discussion between couples, which is necessarily more complicated than any of the above. That's when the cause for the persistence of the tension in your relationship is traceable to an old wound in one partner, usually left over from childhood and often unconscious. Your current dispute is then functioning as a cover for the unspoken issue or wound.

This is an especially important question to consider if one of you tends to personalize and put undue significance on the other's behavior when it simply represents an inconsiderate action or different style of doing something. For example, if he "forgets" to get you an anniversary card and you interpret his forgetting to mean he doesn't love you and the marriage is meaningless, when it's highly possible he simply forgot the date. This is a "red flag" to help you identify a potential old wound. It then becomes important to reflect on your own leftover childhood hurts, especially feelings of abandonment. Did you lose a parent to death or divorce? Such an early loss would make you especially vulnerable to feeling unloved or even unworthy of love.

Essential

Emotions are never wrong or bad. It's how you express an emotion or how you react to your partner's stated feeling that causes conflict.

It's important to separate your own trigger points from the petty issues that are sure to come up in a marriage relationship of any duration. This is what's called "owning your own stuff."

Disagree Agreeably

Your partner's behavior and words can have a huge impact on you and on the stability of the marriage. Often couples carry the wholly unrealistic expectation that they should agree on most things. If they don't, they then view their relationship as flawed, when the real problem is the unrealistic belief they've brought into the marriage. When the level of conflict rises as a result of inflated expectations of marital harmony, both partners often begin to act out with negative behaviors. They hurl insults and blame each other for the nasty state of affairs; they despair and fight on. Often, a couple gets stuck in this trading of negative behaviors and comes to the false belief that it spells the end of their marriage.

Here is the problem: Most marriages stay in this power struggle stage for years and do serious permanent damage to their communication system. The partners develop habits of expressing anger and contempt to each other. Each holds the intent of trying to control his partner, rather than respecting and honoring her.

How to Stop the Negative Behavior

No one would dream of taking a brand new baby and handling it harshly. The same should be true for a new love. It is new, impressionable, and needs tenderness, care, and gentleness. Harsh communication from anger destroys love and builds resentment. Caring communication needs to be present if you want your new love to grow.

 Question

Is there ever one truth when two partners disagree?
Never. The truth in a relationship always has two viewpoints. Therapists are not "relationship police" who judge who is right and who is wrong. There is just your truth and your partner's truth, and together the communal reality is an agreed-upon consensus. Finding a compromise that works for both is the process of achieving harmony and peace within your relationship. Demanding your partner accept your perception as "the truth" only produces a power struggle.

If couples appear to be unconscious of how they sound when talking to each other, Stephen Martin often recommend the two partners make an audio recording of their disagreements and then listen to how they sound. With this "objective evidence" of the negative behaviors right in front of them, the couple can work toward finding new ways to speak that accomplish the task without destroying the love. Just as football players watch game tapes to improve their passing and blocking skills, if couples are serious about building a better marriage the partners can use a replay system to improve their communication skills.

It's important to realize that people have different tolerances for conflict. Some like to blow off steam, and feel better immediately afterward. Some find such verbal venting terrifying. Many others fall somewhere in between these two extremes. One issue to settle early in a marriage is which category you and your partner fall in. If one is a screamer and the other finds such behavior intolerable, you have a serious difference requiring attention and compromise.

Communication is not just what is said, but just as important it includes what is not said. If you have a breakdown in communication, it becomes essential that you immediately fix the problem. If you cannot fix it by yourselves, get outside help. Marital mediation, pastoral couples counseling, or professional marriage therapy are the best professional services to assist you in getting back on course and resuming effective communication.

Chapter 5

Ten Rules of Fair Fighting

IF YOU CHOOSE to be in a committed relationship, you must accept the fact that there will be disagreements between you and your partner. Some of these will escalate into fights. To deal with disagreements in a constructive way, you need to establish rules for fair fighting. Any rules you decide on should be tailored to your unique relationship. Someone who can't tolerate a voice raised in anger (many people) is going to need a rule that both partners use a normal tone of voice when fighting. This chapter contains ten rules of fair fighting along with some examples and explanations of how each rule helps you make your marriage happy.

What Is a Fair Fight?

Fair fights contain a balance of emotion and reason. Before you begin to review these rules, there's one principle you should understand and think about how it applies to you and your marriage. That is, the difference between emotions and reason in marital disagreements. In most human beings, emotions affect decision making more than logic does. So, to handle conflicts you must understand your emotions, and then attempt to add reason to your process.

Sorting Out Emotions and Reason

Most individuals drift between emotions and reason and get confused about which is which. When a woman says "You don't love me anymore," she is offering a "You" message that is also an extreme emotional reaction to something. That something could conceivably be real. If, for example, her partner told her that morning that he is no longer "in love" with her, she is simply restating what he said with her own feeling attached. More likely, her response is provoked by something to which she incorrectly attaches an extreme reaction. For example, she may be bitterly disappointed on her birthday when her husband fails to come home with a gift.

What else might she say that would be more appropriate to the situation? How about, "I'm hurt that you didn't acknowledge my birthday by giving me a token of your love." This "I" message would be both reasonable and appropriate. Especially if, by expressing this feeling, it opens up the subject of gift-giving for this couple to discuss, and what compromises they settle on if they don't see eye to eye.

Finding harmony within a relationship requires that each partner deal first with his emotions and then for both to explore reasonable accommodations or compromises in the marriage—without making either right or wrong, or making the relationship subject to the emotional swings of either partner.

The following ten rules for fair fighting are designed to help you create the boundaries needed to achieve these objectives. They should help you make room for openly acknowledging important emotions that may be lurking behind your behaviors (sometimes feelings you are unconscious of), but then invite in reason and compromise. Boundaries—another word for ground rules—should function as a safety net. If you cannot provide this safety net on your own, you will need an outside mediator to facilitate those disagreements that tend to generate deep emotional responses and destabilize your marriage. Once you've agreed upon your rules, it's a good idea to write them down. Then both sign and date the resulting document as you would any binding agreement.

Rule 1: Keep It Private

Fighting by a married couple in front of other people is embarrassing to those around you and undermines your relationship. A sharp criticism or negative outburst made in front of other people is often a power play by the more verbally skilled spouse, or whichever one does not mind the embarrassment. By fighting in front of in-laws or friends, you risk giving them the impression that your relationship is in perpetual strife. This can then become a self-fulfilling prophecy. You also may get uninvited opinions on the issue under discussion. This will only roil the situation and make agreement more difficult. Resist the impulse to ask others' opinions on your marital disagreements; certainly never call for a vote from whoever happens to be nearby.

 **Alert**

Parents, it's disastrous to fight in front of your children. You must conduct yourselves as a team as much as possible when dealing with kids. Children do not need to hear the content of adult fights. Younger children become fearful as a result of raised voices, particularly if their parents are yelling, crying, or banging on things in front of them. Whatever you do, avoid starting a disagreement in front of your children.

If a fight erupts in front of other adults and especially children, make an immediate agreement to handle it privately at another time.

Rule 2: Schedule Your Arguments

It is always wise to put the request to your partner ahead of time, asking for a time and place to discuss your differences. It's also helpful to advise your partner of the topic you wish to discuss. Many people will have a defensive reaction if they don't receive warning of a potentially difficult discussion. There's no right or wrong involved, defensiveness is just a possible reaction you may as well try to avoid. Requesting an appropriate time for dealing with a disagreement is respectful and supports the resolution of the problem.

> *A request might sound something like this: "We always have disagreements about how to celebrate Christmas. I want to go to my mother's this year. What do you want to do? How can we handle our different desires . . . you want to stay home and I want to bring the kids to visit my family? Christmas is six months away, but if we're going to buy plane tickets we should do it soon. When is a good time to discuss our plans?"*
>
> *Or like this: "You seemed angry that I spent time with my friends after work on Friday night. Can we discuss it on Saturday morning?"*

With advance notice each partner can prepare his thoughts about the issue to be discussed. He can also do some independent sorting out of his own emotions.

Other ways to prepare for the discussion of an issue of contention include:

- Know what you want and how you'll articulate it using an "I" statement
- Be open to what unfolds and don't come with a preconceived notion of what the resolution or compromise is going to be
- Be prepared to own and share your own emotional baggage if there is any that you bring to the discussion
- Think about your bottom line, and what might you be willing to give up in a compromise
- Give some thought to potential compromises, which you can offer as suggestions—not ultimatums

With just a little practice, this type of problem-solving discussion becomes a habit in your marriage. Once established, there will be more trust between you and your partner because each of you can count on having the opportunity to air and deal with a troubling issue in a timely way. Neither of you need sit with a problem and have it fester. The result: more harmony in your marriage.

E ssential

Always think before you speak. To resolve a conflict with a spouse, know what you really want before you ask for anything. You may not get it, but at least you will be clear and honest in your communication.

Rules 3 and 4: Limit the Topic and Stay on Topic

It's easy to let the differences that may exist between you on one issue spread to a number of others, related or not, but this can turn the discussion into a dumping session. Beware: An all-encompassing verbal fight will prevent resolution and it will intensify all the conflicts put "on the table." When this happens, it's far too easy to feel attacked and get into fight-or-flight mode. Unfortunately, neither fighting nor fleeing will get you any closer to solving the difference that began the discussion.

One of the confusing aspects of marital fighting, and a reason why it's sometimes difficult to stay on topic, is that partners rarely are fighting about they think they're fighting about. In fact, many marriage experts agree that most fights are distractions from the real matter stirring up the emotional reactions.

Jack and Christine are attempting to discuss the fact that their household budget is in tatters, but each time they try to tackle it, their discussion degenerates into a shouting match. Here are the ostensible issues. Jack's hours have been cut by the airline he works for; a few months ago, Christine lost her part-time retail job. Without discussing it with Jack beforehand, Christine one recent morning announced her intention not to look any further for a new one, pointing out to Jack the lack of jobs in their area and listing the benefits of her staying home, including her being better able to take care of the kids and cook more meals for the whole family.

Meanwhile, the price of food and gas are up, making money tighter than ever before and pushing their household expenses an average of 20 percent over the amount Jack brings home on a monthly basis. They've been putting the difference on credit cards, but now their cards are maxed out. As the problem worsens, Jack and Christine are fighting over each new bill and blaming each other. Their lowest points come with each bill collector's call; many of these interrupt dinnertime and ruin the meal for everyone. As the situation worsens, Jack's taken to ranting about the problem, often leaving Christine in tears. Otherwise, a tense silence has taken over their communication.

What's going on here? Simply put, Jack and Christine have stopped working together as a team. But things are rarely that simple. Even though this couple's financial deficit is an entirely real and pressing problem, the level of conflict and extreme emotion between them indicates something else at work. The fact that Christine came to the independent conclusion that she would not seek another job without discussing it with Jack was a sign of deteriorating trust and poor communication. If Jack and Christine don't uncover the underlying feelings driving this reoccurring and escalating conflict, they'll never solve their financial issue. In fact, they risk putting the family at greater financial risk.

Fortunately, at this point, Jack and Christine came to couples therapy. At first, each vented their pent-up feelings and beefs about the other. Jack told Christine that she should look more aggressively for another job. Christine expressed her frustration about not finding a new job after looking for several months, and her hurt that Jack didn't value her staying home to be a better mother and wife.

After taking the time to explore his emotions in the safety of a therapist's office, Jack got in touch not only with his anger about carrying the financial burden but also his fear of failing to be able to support his family, and the potential loss of their home if they fell behind on mortgage payments. Jack then looked at how he habitually kept his fears to himself and tended to shut down or get angry rather than ask for emotional support from Christine. When he allowed himself to feel this previously unacknowledged fear, Jack's more vulnerable emotions reached the surface, allowing Christine to meet him at the level of that vulnerability with understanding and compassion. Christine also shared her fears, along with her love and respect for Jack's hard work.

Christine and Jack were then able to get on the same side in this crisis. Only after reaching this place of emotional honesty were Jack and Christine able to address the reality that Jack's salary wasn't sufficient to meet their household needs. If Christine did not find another job, a drastic cut in their household expenses was necessary. They then got to work making those cuts. Christine also agreed to visit a job counselor to look for more part-time employment options. The point for Jack and Christine was that their emotions got entangled with the practical issues, leaving each feeling isolated, overburdened, and alone.

Like so many couples facing similar financial pressures, unless emotions are identified and addressed, practical issues will not get solved—and, if they are, it will only be a temporary fix. Further, when one partner makes important decisions, such as whether or not to continue looking for work, without consulting with her spouse the relationship has entered dangerous territory. This tricky combination of practical and emotional issues will soon destroy a marriage unless the partners raise a red flag and resume working together as a team.

Clearing Emotions

So how do you find out what you are really fighting about? First, you must produce a safe place for an honest discussion to happen. This means clearing the emotions that may be obscuring the issue you're trying to settle. This can be done individually, or if doing so might open you up as a couple to more intimate understanding of each other, try doing it together.

If you simply need to get your own frustration or anger out of the way, many therapists recommend shouting into pillows to let out the rage (and mute the volume), or taking a walk around the block to cool down. The purpose of these activities is to break the intensity of the moment and then come back to the issue as soon as possible. One person in the couple has to begin to defuse the emotion. It is often essential to take a time-out for a short period of time with a specific agreement to get back to the matter once the emotions are in more control.

Some questions for self-reflection when dealing with emotional baggage:

- What feelings are coming up in me that I'm blocking? For example, behind anger there is often fear or sadness lurking.
- If the emotions are tied to an old emotional wound, think about who was the original perpetrator of the hurt? Once identified, you can allow yourself to safely feel the emotions you did not feel as a child. You can also look at the situation from the point of view of whoever caused the hurt, to gain understanding and ultimately acceptance and forgiveness.
- How can I separate what's happening in my marriage from this old hurt? Often just by recognizing the unconscious old wound that was triggered by something said in the present will loosen the tie between present and past. It will also help you and your marriage but only if you can share that old emotional wound with your partner.

Everyone carries childhood hurts into adulthood. A man who had a strong mother and an absent father often carries forward a fear of being emotionally engulfed by his wife. His reaction to strong emotions from her can include withdrawal and shutting down.

 ## Question

How do you know if a fight is tied to an old emotional wound?
The subject of the fight is reoccurring, it's accompanied by extreme aggression by one partner or withdrawal by another, and/or there's a reoccurring, triggering event that produces a strong emotional reaction. These are signs of emotional baggage—e.g. fear of abandonment or fear of being engulfed—resurfacing from the past.

Conversely, a woman whose father was absent during childhood may bring an underlying fear of abandonment into her marital disagreements. When this woman's husband raises his voice or offers a complaint, she may react as a child would out of a fear of being left, rather than as an adult woman addressing the issue at hand. One reason for marriage is to provide a *container* or safe place for each partner's core wounds to be brought to awareness and processed, allowing personal growth both for the individuals and the marriage.

Limit the Topic

As soon as possible, ideally before you start a discussion, try to pinpoint and agree on exactly what you and your partner are fighting about. Then, work toward resolution of only that issue—one topic at a time. When couples are fighting, the real need is for the underlying issue to be brought to the table. However, the underlying issue behind any particular fight is often hard to find. Tensions often occur when transitions happen with a marriage, such as a change in employment status, a new baby, or a suddenly empty nest. These changes put strain on any existing weaknesses in the relationship, and it is these weaknesses that suddenly demand attention. Identifying those stresses that tend to produce fighting in your marriage is a vital part of the communication process.

Fights in times of transition can be a blessing in disguise if they help the couple address an underlying issue that may have been invisible before. Taking one topic at a time helps the couple work their way through to find and deal with that weakness. However, unless and until the underlying issue is located and addressed, you cannot solve the more superficial problem.

Betsy feels strongly that her husband Daniel's friendship with a coworker has gone past what she feels is appropriate for him as a married man and she wants him to terminate the relationship. Daniel protests that he's not being sexual with this coworker, that he simply enjoys hearing this younger woman's perspective on things at work. She's also introduced him to new things, such as a yoga class he's started attending at her suggestion.

For Betsy, a stay-at-home wife and mother whose youngest child has just left for college, this relationship is threatening. Why? Daniel says he loves his wife and does not wish to have an affair with his coworker. Daniel points out that he's resisting his wife's attempt to control his behavior, saying this desire to control him is what's straining the twenty-year marriage, not his friendship with the coworker.

Essentially, Daniel wants to spread his wings; Betsy wants to keep them trimmed. Which of these two partners needs to change his or her behavior to make the marriage work? The answer is both.

In couples therapy, Betsy confronted several things: Her need for a new focus for the energy she previously spent on her now grown children, and her long-standing feeling that Daniel did not share his feelings honestly with her, leaving her wanting for intimate conversation. She acknowledged her fear that Daniel's new friend was getting what she never got in twenty-six years of marriage.

Daniel confronted his passive-aggressive emotional stance in the marriage, which manifested as him staying emotionally distant from Betsy and his not making efforts to spend time exploring new things in the relationship or communicating intimately. With this host of issues, Betsy's jealousy over Daniel's friendship can be seen as a symptom of other underlying issues having to do with communication and intimacy in the marriage. In order for Betsy and Daniel to come to terms with ground rules for outside relationships, they needed to first address what was missing in their marital connection.

As seen in this example, a couple must locate the real issue causing friction and focus on it before attempting to handle another issue, which may be merely a symptom of the underlying problem. If you don't, both issues will only become muddled and more difficult to settle. Often a couple must have the help of a third party to identify what's really going on within a marital dispute under the surface. However, the good news is that once the process of stepping back and taking a deeper look at marital difficulties is learned, the couple can practice it without outside help.

Rule 5: Allow Time-Outs

When a couple has a passionate emotional conflict, the intensity of the argument can become overwhelming. Smart couples establish signals for time-outs, and always establish a time to get back to the discussion after the time-out. A good option is to agree on a hand signal like those used by quarterbacks when they request a time-out during a football game. By far, the hardest dynamic for couples to deal with is voicing negative feelings toward the other partner. Many get lost in negative exchanges, not realizing that the relationship is made of much more than these passing feelings. When decisions are made solely from feelings, people get into serious trouble.

Negative feelings can be very troubling. Someone holding negative feelings about his partner may obsess and worry that nothing can be done about the issue; he fears that she or the situation will never change, bringing him a sense of despair. This compulsive behavior will create stress and can cause physical harm to his body. Learning how to let go of negative thoughts and feelings is vital to happiness and good self-esteem.

 **Alert**

When you're upset with a partner, everything you feel in this state of disequilibrium does not need to be said aloud. "If you let raw sewage in your marriage, don't expect a garden to grow," says Dr. Gary Chapman in his book, *The Marriage You've Always Wanted.*

How Not to Deal with Worry

The challenge is how to let go when your entire being wants to hold on; how do you stop the waves of compulsivity when you cannot find the off switch? Many people turn to alcohol and drugs as a way to self medicate this type of obsessive emotional pain. The danger with this is that it temporarily works, until you sober up and begin having negative feelings again, and then you need another drink to stop feeling.

The key to emotional health is to permit yourself to feel what you are feeling and to ride those feelings like you would a wave in the ocean. Feelings come in waves—the skillful learn how to understand them, and then process these painful episodes so that tranquility can return after the storm. Denial of what is going on within you is the least effective path toward mastering your feelings. Acceptance and understanding of your inner process is the only way to correct the imbalance.

Talking about how you feel is the prudent road to working through the angst. Timing in life is vital. There is a time to talk, and a time to refrain from talking. Knowing when to talk and with whom is a vital part of the path to self-mastery. As may now be increasingly clear, the way to make your marriage work is to find the right balance between talking and holding your tongue, and then determining whether you and your partner can handle the issue alone or whether the better course is to find a third party to help you negotiate a difficult topic either by yourself or jointly with your partner.

Rule 6: Offer Solutions with Criticisms

If you habitually criticize your spouse without offering solutions, you are "garbage dumping" and you will only intensify the hostility between you. The point of all disagreements is to come to resolution, not to overload the relationship with negativity. Here's an exchange where a negative dynamic is at work.

> ***Original criticism:*** *"I can't believe you forgot to take out the trash again this morning. That's so irresponsible."*

> ***Revised criticism with solution:*** *"Unfortunately, you didn't get the garbage can out in time this morning. I was thinking it might be easier to remember to take it out to the curb the night before. What do you think?"*

> *"I'm sorry, I hit the snooze alarm and missed it."*

> *"Should we do something to remind you the night before?"*

> *"No, I'll handle it."*

In order to move one's thoughts or a discussion from complaints to solutions, a positive attitude and a desire for harmony is essential. In other words, you must move away from the "bunker mentality" that makes each of you feel like you're in a battle with the other. In this case, the other is the person you've chosen as your life partner, so this attitude is wholly out of place. At the same time, it's a human tendency to back into a corner and take cover when you feel unheard, unseen, and under attack—even if the incoming artillery is your own negative thinking.

This is where commitment comes into the equation. When you chose to marry, you agreed to attack your differences together, not as two separate competing armies.

Rule 7: Never Say "You Never" or "You Always"

Making generalizations in the form of accusations does not help you work toward resolution of marital disagreements. Rather it intensifies the fighting and leads to deeper emotional hurts. When you find yourself heading toward making such a statement, it's important to put on the brakes. This is exactly the sort of negative, often compulsive thinking that makes it more difficult for you to see your own part in creating the conflict. After all, if everything were always his fault, there would be no room in the dynamic for your fault.

All marital issues have two sides, and each partner is responsible for her side in any conflict in the marriage. If the partner who is more verbally adept makes a habit of regularly criticizing her partner, she risks killing the relationship. The criticized partner will eventually come to the conclusion that he is wrong most of the time, or at least wrong for his current partner. The reality is no one wants to be wrong that often. It's an intolerable situation and it will have to eventually break down—whether into verbal or physical abuse, permanent estrangement, or divorce.

Words Matter

While criticisms of specific aspects of one's behavior are not enjoyable to hear, most people learn to listen and deal with such criticisms when they have to. They cooperate because there's a clear incentive for them to do so. Indeed, this is how all people grow in their social skills, and social interaction is a necessity to human happiness. That said, no one grows from hearing a negative judgment that makes a blanket condemnation of who he is as a person. In fact, such judgments tend to reinforce negative behaviors by encouraging the person to isolate himself from the one doing the condemning. It's natural to defend against negativity.

 Fact

What's the fastest way to make a marital disagreement degenerate into a nasty fight? Tell your partner everything you believe to be wrong with him.

To review and summarize, here are some words guaranteed to escalate a conflict:

- You always (criticize me)
- You never (pick up after yourself)
- You don't (love me anymore)
- You're worse than (my mother, father, boss)
- I wish I'd never (married you, had children with you)

Here are some words guaranteed to de-escalate a conflict:

- I feel (sad about your forgetting our anniversary)
- I need (more affection)
- I'm sorry (for over reacting, my poor choice of words)
- You are right about (my overreaction)
- I regret saying (you don't love me)
- I appreciate your saying (you love me)

In the end, there is nothing more powerful in marriage than the expression of appreciation between partners. Tell your partner you appreciate her. Tell her often.

Rule 8: Set Off-Limit Topics

Everyone is emotionally vulnerable and insecure in some areas. In a healthy marriage you understand your partner's areas of vulnerability and do not hit below the belt by saying things to intentionally trigger these vulnerabilities. That is, unless your true intent is to escalate the hostilities between the two of you. Each spouse needs to let his partner know exactly where his belt line lays. When you are in harmony, you understand that some topics require special handling.

Some typical "no go" areas of discussion with which you may begin your list include: former lovers and spouses, criticisms of parenting styles (particularly when the children are from a former marriage), weight and other aspects of appearance, and any blanket statements that inflame the discussion. This does not mean you never discuss any of these or other below-the-belt areas. It just means you do so with great care.

Essential

When old hurts are triggered in your marriage, shutting down makes you unlovable and unapproachable to your partner. By sharing an emotional wound, you will bring forth enormous compassion and love from your partner. The simple act of sharing opens both your hearts, and makes you lovable and approachable.

When dealing with a below-the-belt topic you should:

- Warn your partner ahead of time that you need to address the topic
- Ask if she's willing
- Acknowledge that it is a difficult topic for her
- Leave judgments out of the discussion as much as possible (It's impossible to have no judgments)

- Know what you need ahead of time in order to let go of the issue
- Stay on topic
- Express your appreciation to your partner for listening

The objective of any conversation on a difficult topic is to accomplish whatever is needed to avoid having to revisit this area repeatedly in the future.

Rule 9: Don't Save Up Anger

Too often, couples arrive for therapy when the hostilities in the marriage have already reached the breaking point. If you are conscious of issues that cause tension in your marriage, it is important to release the complaints gently—without anger—from time to time. Saving up hostilities until emotions are extreme risks catapulting the marriage into disaster.

E**ssential**

People don't make you miserable. You choose to be made miserable. If you feel like your partner is causing your misery, try this two-step process. Step one: Look first at your expectations for marriage. Are they reasonable? Step two: Examine your own part in what's wrong. How can you stop contributing to the negativity? If you're still unhappy, do steps one and two again.

Some of the dangerous ways anger is expressed between partners include:

- Contempt, including sarcasm, cynicism, sniping, and other forms of negativity
- An accusation of a moral deficiency ("You're lazy, self-indulgent, thoughtless")

- Defensiveness ("It's not my fault, it's yours")
- Shutting down, not listening, not responding to a partner's complaint
- Nagging

It's a sure sign of unexpressed anger when your problem-solving exchange immediately escalates into the trading of accusations or another nonconstructive discussion instead of staying on topic.

Expressing Anger Constructively

Everyone feels angry from time to time. It's one of those feelings that can alert you to the fact that something is wrong. The challenge for most people is figuring out what to do with the experience of anger when they feel it. If ignored, anger can eat you up inside and produce disease. Expressed foolishly and carelessly, you may soon be living your life alone, or having a never-ending series of relationships that do not last very long.

Bad ways to deal with anger include:

- Finding someone to dump your anger on. This is the coward's way out of this sometimes-difficult emotion. Someone who gets behind the wheel of a car and expresses his rage by cutting off another driver or honking the horn incessantly is often a person looking for an easy target to let go of rage. This causes accidents and never effectively deals with anger.
- Taking out your rage verbally or physically by abusing those who are weaker. Whether the victim is a spouse, a subordinate employee, or a child, you are behaving as a bully expressing rage toward someone who cannot defend against it.
- Discrimination or prejudice.

All of these are examples of holding defenseless victims responsible for the inner turmoil within the abuser.

There are good and bad ways to deal with anger. Knowing the difference can help make your marriage work. Some good ways to channel anger include:

- Go walking, running, or to the gym. Exercise is the often the best form for releasing overpowering anger.
- Take on a large chore, such as mowing the lawn or cleaning the house.
- Hit, scream, and yell: A punching bag is good. Hitting a mattress can work just as well. Avoid walls. Screaming into pillows or while driving alone in the car also work.

Movement will release the inner tension and help dissipate the pent-up energy inside you. These techniques release the inner tension without picking a fight with a loved one, or doing damage to yourself and others by being reckless with your body. Once you take responsibility for your feelings, they can be managed, reduced, and ultimately eliminated. Anger, like other negative feelings, doesn't need to be nursed along or brought to full expression.

 Question

How can anger be turned into a positive thing in a marriage?
Anger is a powerful emotion that can create necessary change in your life—if it is properly understood, accepted by the one feeling it, and expressed rationally. The energy behind your anger needs to be released, but it's far better to channel it elsewhere rather than dump it on the one you love.

All of the methods for dissipating anger should be viewed as constructive alternatives to dumping anger on your partner—whether the two of you are in the middle of a difficult discussion or not. If you are in a discussion when strong feelings of anger bubble up inside you, this is when you should call a time-out; then always agree on a time to resume. (Not to resume is to avoid.) Remember, anger is not constructive or helpful in getting to the resolution of any disagreement.

Rule 10: The Art of the Apology

Why is it so hard to say, "I'm sorry?" Often it's because you've gotten overly invested in being "right." If you can't apologize, it's a sign that being right has overtaken the goal of restoring harmony to your relationship. Plus, if you're always right, your partner must always be "wrong." Why would you wish to be in relationship with a person who's always wrong?

Answer: Because you are competing with your partner, not sharing a life together. Flexibility in human relationships is essential.

Tolerance for personality differences, individual preferences, and just plain bad days make the difference between a marriage enduring or falling apart. Successful couples value harmony above the ego's need to win. In happy relationships the partners place a very high value on flexibility. And when differences arise, these couples search for the win/win solution as opposed to the win/lose outcome.

 **Alert**

Never, ever, threaten divorce if you don't mean it. Nothing good can come of such a threat. Using divorce as an ultimatum will only blow up a marital fight, and preclude conflict resolution.

Teamwork, Not Competition

Sporting contests work best with a winner and a loser, but this is not true of marriages. Handling marital differences requires tolerance for individual differences, a sense of humor to laugh at absurdity, and forgiveness to move beyond the pain.

Marriages have to handle the speed bumps of life. It is unrealistic to demand that life serve you up only good days. It is how the couple handles the difficult experiences that determines the success or failure of marriage—not how well they handle their best days together. Relationships are not a contest; they are a support system. Unlike sports, when competition enters a marriage, the relationship sours.

Letting go of issues—deciding they are not the deal breakers you once thought they were—will strengthen your marriage bond. All successful relationships actively practice the art of forgiveness and humor, so whenever the going gets tough they can more easily find the way to laughter instead of fighting. Successful couples surrender into harmony, love, and the joy of becoming one. As the poet Ogden Nash said, "Whenever you're wrong admit it, whenever you're right, shut up."

Chapter 6

Marriage and Money: The Fault Lines

IF YOUR MARRIAGE is a happy one, you've probably figured out how to manage your finances together. If you're not there yet, this is the chapter where you consider why. Money problems tear marriages apart faster than any other single issue. The fault lines that weaken marital ties can usually be traced to a lack of solid agreements between spouses on some key issues: your joint values and financial priorities, who will be responsible for minding the money, and how you'll deal with the inevitable "surprises" that sap the best laid plans. Before getting to money management solutions in Chapter 7, it's important to understand the sources of weaknesses in your marital money system.

Finances as a Power Issue in Marriage

Janice and Brad married in their early thirties, after he'd worked his way up to top producer in high-tech sales, while she found herself stuck in bottom rung marketing jobs. Because they lived in the same high-cost metropolitan area, Janice had collected debts—car and student loans, credit cards totaling over $10,000, and a medical bill she was still paying off—prior to the marriage, which she then brought into it. In the beginning, Brad, much in love, agreed to take on Janice's debts, saying he didn't mind helping her pay them off. The couple then co-mingled their finances into the standard (although problematic) one pot approach to marital money management.

While one partner taking on another's debts is not uncommon, it adds an imbalance to a new marriage, which can quickly create tension and foster manipulation of one partner by the other who may use money as an instrument of power. By the time Janice and Brad arrived in couples therapy, just two years into the marriage, her primary complaint was that Brad criticized her "constantly," while Brad's complaint was their dormant sex life. In this relationship, Janice, an attractive and bubbly young woman, had the superior social and verbal skills, while Brad nursed insecurities about his social awkwardness. Brad's superior financial position, and the fact that he'd accepted Janice's past debts, had become the instruments by which he attempted to control his wife. The fact that Brad and Janice's sex life had become dormant was a likely indication of Janice's anger at Brad. Janice disliked her financial dependence on Brad, so she unconsciously punished him for the power this gave him over her by withholding sex. Brad was unnerved when Janice removed her affection, since her adoration permitted him to avoid his own feelings of low self-esteem.

 **Alert**

When they marry, many young people find themselves—for the first time—accountable to another person for their money habits. Adding to this adjustment, expenses often rise sharply once a household of two (or three) is established, making smart money management not a choice but an absolute necessity. It's a time fraught with tensions and mistakes. You will be able to learn if you both make honesty your number one priority.

While it's legitimate to view the financial problems in a troubled relationship such as this one as symptoms of deeper issues, Janice and Brad's money issues soon took on a life of their own and became a force of destruction inside the marriage. Because the dynamics evident in their story are typical of marriages within the first five years, it's vitally important to recognize how they can strain relationships, and then take steps to lessen these pressures. Starting a marriage with money problems is like exposing a fragile seedling to a drought. Its growth will be stunted; worse, it may wither and die.

Your Family Money Legacy

One of the main factors determining your money style as an adult is how your parents handled family finances while you grew up and see how your style may compare to theirs. Everyone doesn't respond exactly the same to the same set of childhood circumstances. If your family of origin faced economic hardships, as an adult you could respond by developing a tendency to spend like there's no tomorrow to compensate for feelings of deprivation you may have had as a child, or conversely by hoarding every penny in fear of facing the same fate. It's important to take a close look at where you came from since parents are the primary models for joint money management for most people.

The most important piece of information to draw from a family history is your own "money story." Was there a big emphasis on saving when you were growing up? Was this Mom's or Dad's idea or both? Did one parent counterbalance the other's money stance—for instance, did Mom hide "pin money" to compensate for Dad's impulse buying? If so, whose "side" did you take, overtly or not? Each person has a story around money created by his upbringing, and how he's dealt with money as an adult before the marriage, as well as the consequences of those actions, which may still be present in his life.

Figuring Out Your Money Story

- Did you receive an allowance as a child? What did you do to earn it?
- When did you get your first paycheck? Did you spend or save some of it?

- Were there fights over money in your parents' marriage?
- What is your history with spending and saving?
- Do you ever spend or save as an emotional reaction? For example, you have a fight with your partner and immediately go to the mall and buy a new outfit. Or, you have a dispute with your coworker and decide to cut back on the family food budget. In both cases, money is being used as an emotional fix, not as a rational reflection of your household budget priorities.
- Are you by nature a risk taker or risk averse? How does this translate into your money style? It's possible that you take more physical than financial risks, for example, by mountain climbing or playing extreme sports. You could apply the same taste for risk to more than one area, including money, by gambling, day trading in the stock market, or investing in a new business. All of these activities share one result: They produce adrenalin rushes for the risk taker. In many cases, the purpose of these rushes is to allow the risk taker to avoid his emotions, either the unpleasant feelings he has in the present or painful ones from the past.

Share Your Money Legacies

When you are finished compiling your own money story, it is imperative that you share it with your partner and encourage him to share his with you. By figuring out how you are similar or differ in money styles, you have important data to use in drawing up marital agreements and responsibilities around finances. For example, the detail-oriented partner who enjoys bookkeeping is the logical choice for the role of hands-on bill payer. The person whose file drawer looks like a trash can is not.

It's also essential for married couples to agree on their financial goals. It's amazing how many young and middle-aged couples avoid coming to terms with different views on where their combined money should go. This would be like getting in the car and filling up the tank with gas but not having a destination for your journey. Do you want to make saving for your child's college education your number one priority? What trade-offs are you willing to make between your children's needs and saving for your own retirement? Will you travel widely or spend vacations with family?

E ssential

While it makes sense to select the partner with the better book-keeping skills to handle the family books on an ongoing basis, it's also a good idea to occasionally trade roles. Give the one who tends to spend and not record checks the job of reconciling the monthly income and expenses. Have him then present the results to his partner. Learning and behavior modification are more likely to take place by doing.

One partner's personal dreams can play a big part in his wants and needs for money in the marriage. Does he dream of retiring early in order to paint landscapes up and down the Pacific coastline? Such dreams may be fragile, or unconscious, and they are also often unexpressed between two people in a long-term marriage. Without knowing where you want to end up, it's impossible to select the right course to get there.

Who's the Spendthrift, Who's the Miser?

Opposites attract. It's the only possible explanation for why spend-thrifts and misers tend to marry each other. Any marriage therapist will tell you it's true, since this is the combination of personality types they see in their offices on a regular basis dealing with marital money strife. As to why these opposites continue to attract, one could imagine an evolutionary instinct encouraging people to balance their extreme tendencies with the opposite quality. That is, if you tend to compulsively spend, you seek out a compulsive saver to ensure your survival.

Whether this human drive for balance in money styles exists from a scientific perspective is unknown, but it appears to be an unconscious drive for partners in mate selection. Your challenge is to balance each other's more extreme tendencies. Of course, the combination of two extremes does not ensure balance in money management or anything else. It does, however, ensure friction and conflict if not addressed.

Who Is the Spendthrift?

Put simply, he is the one who spends more money than he has in his pocket or bank account. He's the person who buys things for emotional reasons, or on impulse. He may spend money in order to get external approval based on the things he owns rather than who he is as a person. The spendthrift can also be motivated by a love of risk, with high-risk investments or gambling involved in the games of risk he plays as a way to keep his adrenalin high. A spendthrift will insist on staying in only four-star hotels on a vacation with his wife so he can enjoy the sense of status he gets in the glances of fellow lodgers, rather than focusing on how he'll balance the couple's budget for the rest of the vacation.

 Fact

According to a 2008 online survey of 74,000 men and women, about half of all couples said they fight about money at least once a month. Contrary to conventional thinking, couples also said that big money fights rarely lead to steamy make-up sex.

Who Is the Miser?

A miser gets emotional satisfaction or a feeling of enhanced security from not spending her money or by doing without. A miser denies herself things that others might consider necessities, for example, fresh fruit at meals, in addition to obvious luxuries, such as caviar or champagne. She may be attempting to alleviate a free-floating sense of guilt or an underlying feeling that she does not deserve the "good things in life." Some call this attitude a "poverty mentality," where an individual deals with an intense fear of not having enough by not indulging in anything that might not be deemed essential.

Either in Moderation

The problems with both of these money temperaments lay in their extremes. Either set of traits in moderation could represent an entirely appropriate approach to marital money management.

It's possible that neither you nor your partner has an extreme money style. Maybe you are a mix of both tendencies, perhaps at different times and under different conditions. The important process to accomplish by the end of this chapter is to identify your dominant tendencies regarding money and see how you impact each other. Do you help each other avoid facing financial realities by both indulging in overspending? Does one of you grin and bear it while watching the other overspend, all the while saving up anger and resentment? These terms are presented to help you reflect and take responsibility for your actions, not to blame each other or provoke conflict.

 **Alert**

Compulsive saving, or hoarding, can be as destructive to financial stability and marital harmony as compulsive spending. Hoarding often reflects a person's obsessive reaction to an underlying anxiety or fear, such as a fear of abandonment or not having enough based on an unresolved childhood trauma. The only way to deal positively with money in marriage is to free it from all hidden attachments and agendas.

He Makes the Money, She Spends It

These next three sections describe different household money management models with specific issues and challenges tied to the question of which partner serves as breadwinner. It's another area of marriage, like the legal status of women discussed in Chapter 2, that remains in confusion and flux after decades of intense change. Today, 61 percent of married women work outside the home. That means 39 percent of married women do not. Their reasons for staying home vary. Perhaps a woman is unable to find a job, or she and her spouse made a joint decision that she stay home to care for children or an elderly relative, or the husband earns sufficient salary for the household. Regardless of the specific reason, in this first model the household depends primarily on the traditional family structure of a single male breadwinner.

 Fact

The past century has seen a huge increase in the number of married women working outside the home. According to the U.S. Census, between 1955 and 2005, labor force participation by married women rose from 30 to 61 percent, with the largest change occurring between 1970 and 1990.

Despite the fact that the number of households where the husband earns all the family income while his wife stays home is now a minority, the cultural stereotype that extols its virtues remains in place. At its least accurate or helpful, this stereotype paints a picture of a hardworking husband slaving to bring home the bacon, while his self-indulgent wife spends her time thumbing through catalogs to find ways to spend *his* money. This negative slant on the single male breadwinner household, if it ever existed outside of classic TV sitcoms, is archaic and yet it persists. Why?

In part, it's because America's cultural perceptions on personal economic matters often lag far behind the financial realities of the majority of its citizens. For example, the fact that real household income has not kept pace with inflation for the last two decades is rarely factored into discussions about why people don't save more.

It's also not helpful that money (like sex) has long been considered a taboo subject for polite conversation, even within families.

The issue here is not whether men and women should or shouldn't desire the traditional model of the single male breadwinner. The problem lies with the negative consequences that stem from setting up a family money system that doesn't reflect the financial realities by which husbands and wives actually live. Two common mistakes that result from this disconnect between reality and fantasy are:

- **Mistake 1:** Handing over the purse strings to the primary breadwinner

Ignorance is not bliss. By not fully engaging in the family finances, a stay-at-home spouse can set herself up for hardships, such as a husband's extravagant spending outside of her purview. Both partners should attend meetings with insurance agents, accountants, financial planners, and lawyers. Nonworking wives should also look over monthly bank statements and credit-card bills. Couples should also make a list of all bank and brokerage accounts and insurance policies and keep it with other important documents, such as wills and medical directives.

- **Mistake 2:** Losing your (financial) identity

The woman who doesn't bring home a paycheck can make the mistake of not establishing credit in her own name. The reality is that after not having your own individual credit cards for a period of six months, credit bureaus are unwilling to calculate your credit score as an individual. This leaves a spouse vulnerable to having no credit identity when she's on her own due to divorce or death of a partner. It is considered wise financial planning for each spouse to maintain separate credit cards regardless of who makes the money.

A Changing Money Model

The consequences of being rigidly tied to outmoded stereotypes for household money management can be negative for the breadwinner, too. In a 2008 online survey of 74,000 men and women on the subject of work, a quarter of the men in the survey said their wives were not working outside the home. Of these respondents, 40 percent said he wished his wife did. Of the approximately 75 percent of men whose wives worked outside the home, only 5 percent said they wished she was at home.

These data support a reality that marriage therapists see in their offices on a daily basis: Many men are harboring unexpressed feelings, including resentment, about handling the lion's share of breadwinning duties. One reason for their reticence to express such feelings and thus clear the air and come to a more satisfactory distribution of marital responsibilities is the traditional view of marriage in which the man must shoulder the sole responsibility for earning the household income. These issues may end up being settled by the changing economy, which is once again making it necessary for both partners in the marriage to contribute to household income just to make ends meet.

E ssential

The number of mothers working outside the home is now trending downward. According to the U.S. Census, married mothers of infants working outside the home (part time, full time, or looking for work) peaked in 1998 at 58.7 percent and decreased to 53.7 percent in 2004. The number of working mothers of older children, which stood at 63 percent in 2000, fell to 60 percent in 2003.

She Makes the Money, He Spends It

Just as the previous money model carries cultural baggage and financial repercussions, this one also comes with its own pitfalls and potential negative consequences. Fortunately, society appears to be moving away from the once common disapproval of the wife who earned more than her husband. However, critical judgments persist toward the husband who stays home to care for children while his wife goes to work. The wife's higher breadwinner status can be seen as a threat to her partner's manhood.

 Fact

According to the U.S. Labor Department, 25.5 percent of wives earned more than their husbands in 2005. This number was up by 17.8 percent since 1987.

The attitudes of men and women appear to be undergoing pervasive change on these issues. After decades of being conditioned to believe that men relish the role of primary provider, an online survey's researchers were surprised to discover that only 12 percent of the men surveyed said they would mind if their wife earned more money than they did. In general, those men who said they wouldn't mind a wife earning more seemed happy to share the breadwinner role. In fact, a full 35 percent of men and 40 percent of women surveyed said a key benefit of having a spouse make money is that it alleviates the pressure of being the only financial provider. While not scientific, these data point to real attitudinal change that appears to now be underway.

Both Make the Money, Both Spend It

This is the financial model seen most often in today's new marriages, whether due to personal preference, economic necessity, or both. If the couple has children, usually the woman takes off time from her career to stay home. However, most of these women (60 percent) plan to return to part-time or full-time work when the child enters day care or school. When two people in a marriage are working outside the home and comanaging a household (with children) they confront a host of money management challenges that test their teamwork and communications skills as well as their commitment to the marriage.

The key to managing this money model is coordination. In the next chapter there are specific recommendations for setting up both joint and separate bank accounts, budgeting, and how to monitor joint and separate spending.

For this money model to work there must be total honesty, deep self-knowledge by each person, and regular in-depth discussions between the two partners. Whereas in all three of these marital money models each partner makes himself vulnerable by allowing the other access to all his financial resources, his credit, and his future dreams, when both make and spend the money, the playing field of risks and opportunities to succeed is level. Each trusts the other to hold up her end of the bargain, because the household's survival depends on both keeping their jobs, picking up the kids at day care, sharing the housework, and somehow having enough energy left at the end of the day to enjoy a marital relationship. This doesn't mean the partners can't and shouldn't divide up responsibilities between them, but there are more fault lines in this model, more balls in the air.

When Your Money Issues Show Up in Other Places

Money problems show up more often and in many more ways than people recognize. In marriages, stress over money can wreak havoc with a couple's sex life without the topic ever coming up for discussion —as it did in Brad and Janice's relationship discussed earlier in this chapter. It also can dampen emotional honesty, and make your household a generally miserable place to be. That's because the often unspoken, underlying dynamic is about power.

When one person is the primary breadwinner, or if one brought substantial money into the marriage, it's very easy for that person to wield power by trying to control his partner's behavior, or by criticizing her. The person who doesn't bring in the money then tends to attempt to manipulate her partner either by withholding sex or emotional support from the more powerful one. The only way out of these negative psychodynamics is through honest reckoning.

Danger Signs of Marital Money Problems

- Purchasing something substantial without consulting partner
- No communication about money
- Unexplained fatigue due to emotional stress
- Denial of family time due to excess overtime hours worked
- Sudden, large increases in credit card balances
- Secretive purchases
- Self-indulgent shopping ("retail therapy")
- Parental loans
- Episodes of depression

Many of these behaviors and personality changes could have multiple causes, but if you see several at once coupled with any indication of money issues, it's time to find a time and place to discuss these concerns with your partner. While there are times when buying on credit is necessary, too often couples avoid confronting the fact that they simply can't afford something by using plastic. When times are tough, the worst possible response is to avoid the hard facts. Debt, like a toothache, won't improve without treatment and a change in behavior.

Chapter 7

Making Money Work in Marriage

AFTER COMPARING YOUR money stories and agreeing on your present household money model, you are ready to take the other essential steps if you are going to make money work in your marriage. These next objectives include defining the money values you have in common, agreeing on financial goals, and establishing a working budget that you can both live with. Think of this process as the blueprint for envisioning and creating your present and future lives together.

Finding Common Money Values

In this process you and your partner will discover what matters most to you, alone and together, now and into the future. Your choices reflect who you are and what you choose to make important in your lives. There are no right or wrong choices. Perhaps for the first time in your life, you must reach consensus with another person on where you'll focus your intent, time, and financial resources. In a marriage, your individual choice must complement and support your partner's if the partnership is going to be harmonious. Think of this process as a unique opportunity through which you can gain the total support of another person for your calling, and then do the same for the person you love.

To be of most use, your common money values should look ahead five, ten, and even twenty years. Many couples elect to make children and family their priority while others opt out of parenthood. Even within the choice to be a parent there is the opportunity to reflect your particular values if you are called to adopt or be a foster parent. Then there's the all-important issue of timing. For example, if one partner chooses to be the only breadwinner so the other can attend or return to college full time, there are short- and long-term consequences. In the short term you both give up time and money, and perhaps delay having children. In the long term this choice provides financial and other benefits for all concerned.

Essential

Smart couples draw up a "financial priority statement" representing their short- and long-term goals for the money they accumulate and spend in the course of the marriage. To compose your statement, you'll need to devote several discussions to the process and arrive at your goals jointly, then treat it as a binding marital contract. This agreement should then be the starting place for all of your money decisions in the marriage.

There is probably no more important single "brick" in building the foundation for your marriage than making clear and careful decisions on your common money priorities. Like any other legal instrument, this agreement should be considered irrevocable until both parties reassess, discuss, and change it.

What Goes into a Financial Priority Statement?

A priority statement is all about creating a hierarchy of importance for the limited amount of time, money, and other resources available to the two of you as a married couple. For each priority you arrive at, there are attendant money and time implications that must also be factored together.

Among the priorities and related issues to be considered are:

- Will you have children? How many?
- If yes, how will childcare be arranged and paid for?
- Does higher education help you advance a financial goal? Will you take turns attending college or job training?
- If one partner is unhappy in his current profession, but a change would require further schooling and/or less salary, is the other partner willing to make the "sacrifice" required?
- If yes, will you pay cash for the schooling or take out student loans and both commit to paying them off over the next five, ten, or twenty years?
- Will you buy a home or rent? How much of your income(s) are you willing to devote to rental or mortgage payments? (Experts suggest no more than 38 percent of family income should go to housing costs.)
- Does an employer provide health care insurance coverage? If not, how will you deal with medical and dental costs? Is a lower cost, higher deductible plan a reasonable alternative in order to cover you against "catastrophic" illness but not present an impossible financial burden?
- What about saving and emergency planning? Financial experts recommend saving 10 percent on a monthly basis and having four to six months of living expenses in reserve. Many people live paycheck to paycheck and consider such a plan "pie in the sky." In the event of a lost job or medical emergency, where will you go for help?

 **Alert**

Money matters far more than most newlyweds think it does or should in a marriage. Never underestimate the potential of shared money values to bring harmony to your relationship, and never ignore the potential of financial disarray to undermine it.

Plan Ahead to Save Money and Marital Stress

Just reading the list of priorities and choices can be exhausting, but that's not a reason to avoid dealing with each and every question. To get through the process, it's a good idea to schedule several discussion times with your partner.

 Question

When is less (money) more in a marriage?
When a couple decides to reduce the stress associated with overworking, commuting, or other money worries related to having a bigger house in favor of having more togetherness or family time. There is no right or wrong in this debate. It is a highly personal set of decisions, which should be part of any couple's financial value statement.

The idea is to think ahead, not wait for a crisis (or unplanned event) to arrive in order to address whether, for example, having a child is more important to you than owning a house. Contrary to popular thinking, no one makes a better decision when her back is against the wall compared to when she has the time to reason, assess her feelings, and carefully consider all variables with her partner. In most cases, two heads really are better than one.

 **Alert**

You may be able to "have it all" in life—children, career, community or national service, spiritual practice, sport, travel, and/or intellectual pursuit—but you cannot have it all at the same time. Choices must be made, priorities assigned, and dreams deferred.

How to Assess Your Spending Needs

Before you can figure out how much money you must allot to each of the items on your list of life priorities, you must take a hard look at how you currently spend your money. To do this, get out six months worth of bank and credit card statements, and any other receipts you keep. This is probably something you've done to prepare your taxes in the past year, and so the records should be available either online or in a box or file. That doesn't mean this part of the process will be easy or pleasant.

Essential

Money conflicts are always about money and something else. Typical underlying issues in financial fights include trust, self-worth, control, and independence. To solve a marital money problem, look closely at your feelings and your partner's to pin down the real issue.

The hard part is accountability—first to yourself, then to your partner. To look on the positive side, there is a relief that comes with facing the truth. It's also the only way to make a change—by starting with where you are right now. This documentation process will help you refine your discussion of common money values. For example, what if one of you considers gym membership a necessity, while your partner views it as a luxury? He suggests you can just take a vigorous morning walk in the park instead of spending $50 a month running on the treadmill. You say that going to the gym is the only way you've been able to keep your commitment to exercise; that it allows you fewer excuses to skip it. Who's right? Well, of course that depends on where exercise fits into your hierarchy of priorities. Not whether exercise is good for you, since that's a given, but what it means for *you*—your health, your state of mind or body. Only then can you and your partner assess its status as an essential or a luxury, and then only in relationship to where else that $50 a month may need to go.

Beware the Miscellaneous

So, if you have all your bill statements and receipts out on the table, you can either use a computer bookkeeping program or do the same thing on a pad of paper, as long as you make a complete list of where your money goes now. In addition to the groupings that are indisputably essential—housing, food, medical care, and clothing—pay special attention to the all-important category called "miscellaneous," otherwise known as the black hole of budgeting.

Take a hard look at the number of lattes, lottery tickets, or down-loadable tunes each of you may purchase in the course of any given week or month. For most people, this is the category that determines whether you're living within a budget or not. These are likely to become the obvious candidates for budget cutting. By extension, they're where most of your money disagreements and tensions will originate.

The Three-Pot Approach: His, Hers, and Ours

Many couples operate using one household bank account for all purposes. Into this one account both route their paychecks. Out of this one account, they pay for all joint and individual bills along with any impulse purchases each may make. They do this by each carrying a separate checkbook for this account, each writing checks or using an ATM for cash and (hopefully) recording these purchases in separate check registers. Many couples also operate in a similar way with jointly held credit cards. Unfortunately, this approach is often an unmitigated disaster.

The main reason is the difficulty of keeping a running balance of the money going out and coming into a bank account or credit card when two people are using it both while they're together and when they're apart. Even with good communication by the partners, it's a system fraught with potential errors and omissions.

His, Hers, and Ours

When applied to household money management, the "his, hers, and ours" approach calls for two separate joint checking accounts, ideally both free of checking fees with a low or no minimum balance requirement. Each partner has primary responsibility for writing checks and balancing one of these two accounts, although legal ownership of the two accounts would reside with both partners in the event access to an account was necessary without the other being present.

This approach limits the amount of ongoing coordination between the two but requires more advance planning. The two partners agree to designate certain incoming monies to go into each checking account. The primary account holder of those accounts would then be responsible for paying certain bills. One pays the mortgage, the other pays the babysitter, and so on. With this arrangement, there is shared responsibility with each focused on different incoming and outgoing monies. Each partner also must balance his own checkbook. At regular meetings, the two review spending and make any necessary adjustments.

The Point of "Pin Money"

This expression originally signified the money given by a husband (who made all the money and spent it, too) to his wife for small personal expenditures such as pins, which were very costly items in centuries past. Today, it refers also to small amounts of money given to anyone—for instance, a spouse, children, or an employee—for incidental expenses over which the users have discretion and thus do not need prior approval to spend on a given item.

This idea can come into play when spouses are using either a one-pot or two-pot system of money management. If possible within either system, it is often a good idea to give each partner some discretionary money from the common funds so that a couple's joining together of financial resources doesn't rob each of a feeling of autonomy within the marriage.

Not having separate discretionary monies available to both partners can lead to tensions and fights, especially when one partner makes solo purchasing decisions and doesn't tell her partner. If she keeps such purchases secret, there is the risk of undermining trust within the relationship. By agreeing to have separate discretionary accounts, a husband and wife are not saying that it's okay to have either of them make major spending decisions autonomously. This plan simply gives both some individual spending prerogatives. Think of it as breathing room.

 **Alert**

The lack of discretionary money for either partner puts an unnecessary stress on a marriage. No one likes to feel powerless over his or her life or purchases.

Making a Budget Stick

At this point you have agreed on your money values and reviewed your current spending. You've also decided whether you'll work with a single or two-pot money management system. It's now time to create a working budget, which will become the bible for day-to-day and month-to-month money management in your household. The following items are in most household budgets. Perhaps obvious, they are listed here to help couples complete the process without forgetting something important.

Be sure each of the following items falls on the list for payment from one of your money pots:

- Mortgage or rent payment
- Food. All in one or divided into two shopping lists? It is a good idea to begin with menus, and create a shopping list from those; however, this may simply not be your style of

meal preparation. If money gets tight, you can view this as an area to return to for refinement.

- Car loan payments, gas, maintenance, car insurance (or public transportation)
- Home or renter's insurance
- Utilities
- Health insurance, out-of-pocket medical and dental costs
- Taxes
- Student loan payments
- Savings, child's education, or retirement plan contribution

Where you place credit card payments within a budget is an important decision. If you are able to pay off the balance on a purchase made that month, then the full amount should go in the category where it logically falls—clothing, gasoline, and so on—since your method of payment should not be the issue. However, if you are carrying forward credit card balances, you have no recourse but to set up an essential (not discretionary) category for debt repayment. Your goal should be to pay more than the minimum balance each month so as to avoid being stuck with runaway interest charges and a perpetually high credit balance. Then there are common discretionary items, which may or may not be deemed essential in your household:

- Haircuts, manicures, beauty treatments
- TV, cable, or satellite TV
- Internet service
- Vacations
- Entertainment (eating out, movies, live events)
- Tuition for education or training courses
- Books, magazines
- Gym or other club memberships or sports activities
- Private school or extracurricular costs for children
- Church or other charitable donations
- One-time costs (health, auto repair, family loan, and so on). It's a good idea to have a budget category that accounts for the inevitable financial surprises in any household.

So you have a budget. Congratulations. However, if you're like most couples, this is when the crushing realization strikes that your total of budgeted costs exceeds your available joint income. This is the time to make cuts. Too often couples reach this point and give up, deciding to put the shortfall on credit and hope for the best . . . meaning more overtime, a raise, a second job, a loan, or something else not tangible. This is like sticking your head in the sand and refusing to see reality for what it is. It's also a sure route to marital disharmony, high stress, and stress-related illness.

The widespread personal and collective financial problems in the United States—families losing homes to foreclosures, the household credit crisis—have largely been the result of people ignoring reality (such as the fine print on loan documents) and hoping for the best (for example, rising home values, better jobs). If you've been a party to this faulty thinking, you're not alone. As the country wakes up to what it has brought down on itself, so too must each household do the same. Part of the challenge of harder economic times is the need to plan ahead for financial crises without knowing when they may strike. With higher unemployment and more job layoffs across many industries, more and more households and marriages are being put to tough tests.

Once you and your partner arrive at a real, workable budget where income matches expenses, you must each keep a copy close by and review it regularly. Then at regular money management sessions, you must examine where your money has gone and keep each other accountable to the commitments you've made. It's no different than what happens (or should happen) in any small or large business.

Marriage as a Family Business

Married couples can learn a lot from how businesses operate. The amount of money going in and out of a typical U.S. household, the challenges of managing and maximizing assets (the two of you as wage earners, your home, savings, vehicles, loans, and income), as well as the monitoring of costs, are not so different than those of a small (or medium-sized) family business. There are also similar pitfalls and solutions to be borrowed from the family business model for married couples.

E ssential

Family businesses, including husbands and wives running a business together, account for 60 percent of all U.S. employment, meaning enterprises where two or more family members own and control the business. Family businesses keep their debt levels lower than other commercial enterprises. They also supply 65 percent of all wages and 78 percent of new jobs, according to a 2004 study.

If your marriage includes a business enterprise on top of the management of your household accounts, your potential for conflict and reward are even higher than faced by most married couples. The similarities are striking. Whether you manage a household or the corner dry cleaner, a restaurant, a tech start-up, or a chain of retail stores, you face the challenges of keeping cash flowing when financial times are bad, negotiating with suppliers or creditors, and managing yourself as well as your other employees.

Probably the most valuable parallel between business and marriage can be seen in the challenge of communication. Not too many businesses would survive without regular meetings to monitor costs and spending and address operational problems. These practical challenges are not significantly different than those that exist in any long-term marriage.

The Long-Distance Marriage

Sometimes, two employed spouses can't find work in the same city, and they must live apart temporarily, maintaining two households but still cooperating on money management and all other aspects of married life from a distance. The primary motivation for living apart while married is financial, with either short- or long-term benefits at stake for the couple. The most common reasons for the choice are career advancement, education (often graduate school), and military deployment. Interestingly, the problems of couples in long-distance relationships are not so different than couples living together, and neither are the solutions. The greatest challenges are keeping up communication between partners and maintaining a balance between work and the relationship.

 Fact

Couples living apart represented 2.9 percent of all U.S. marriages, or 3.6 million people in 2005. This number grew by 30 percent since 2000 with most of the increase attributable to the growth in women's career opportunities putting more couples in the position of having to make a geographic compromise.

According to a 2004 study of 200 married couples living apart done by Purdue University's Center for the Study of Long-Distance Relationships, the average couple in this representative sample lived apart for fourteen months and saw each other one and a half times a month. They reported speaking on the phone with their partners every 2.7 days. Interestingly, this study showed that partners in marriages living apart were not more likely to have extramarital affairs, and these marriages showed no difference in divorce rates.

Other challenges faced by couples in a long-distance marriage include:

- Maintaining interrelatedness (the feeling of being a couple)
- Tendency to avoid difficult topics for discussion during brief periods of togetherness

- The limitations of phone communication (that is, without visual cues) make nuances harder to grasp and arguments harder to resolve
- Limited times for sexual intimacy; different comfort levels with "phone sex" and the tendency to make times together more like a vacation than "real life"

With the complexities and myriad demands of modern life affecting all marriages, there are lessons to be learned in the special challenges faced by those in long-distance marriages. At the risk of sounding like a broken record, it bears noting that, above all else, the quality of communication between partners is the make-or-break element that determines whether these relationships succeed or fail.

Chapter 8

Marriage and Sex

LOVING IS MUCH bigger than sexuality. Loving does not need sexuality, but sexuality, to be fully experienced, needs love. Sexual, sensual, erotic love is the glue that bonds two people in relationship. At its best, your sexuality is a physical, emotional, and spiritual experience—the complete joining of two into one. Like money, however, sexuality is often the site of power struggles in marriage. To keep sex from becoming a bargaining chip in your relationship, you need to give it a sacred, inviolable place in your lives. You need to make it a vital topic for ongoing, intimate communication.

Creating Intimacy and Sexuality

Vulnerability is the only path to sexual intimacy. The woman is always more vulnerable in a heterosexual relationship because she must receive her partner into her body. Nothing could be more vulnerable or beautiful than this invitation. It is both a spiritual act and an expression of surrender. It is also her choice to give herself freely to her partner, which makes the sexual act possible. However, for the experience of sexual intimacy to broaden and become the glue for a long-term marriage, both partners must become vulnerable.

The French refer to the sexual climax as *le petit morte*, the little death. They equate orgasm to a heightened spiritual experience that is similar to death. In death, humans surrender their very essence. In sexual behavior, couples surrender their individuality and enter a sacred realm where the union of two bodies, two hearts, and two souls is possible. Not only is sexuality one of the greatest pleasures of human existence and nature's way to reproduce the human species, but it can also be one of the most healing aspects of a distressed relationship.

Honest conversation about sexual expression is imperative if you want sex to be a healing element in your marriage. Too many couples are afraid to talk about sex, and the results are assumptions and expectations that, if not discussed, will harm the relationship. It becomes essential that if you are sexual, you must also be able to give voice to your sexual needs, desires, and wishes, and you must listen to your partner in a receptive, loving way.

The smart couple does not allow the sacred space of sexuality to be hurt; they protect their sex because of its power and healing quality. Once sex is abandoned or disturbed in a relationship, emotional healing must occur if the couple is to continue to enjoy intimacy. Yet most couples are sexually and emotionally immature. The intense feelings that arise when two people are sexual, or conversely if one partner is withholding sex from the other, are so powerful that too many have no idea how to manage the intensity or the anger.

Same Need, Different Ways to Ask

A man and a woman may both want intimacy with each other, but they will often use different words to ask for what they want. See if you can guess who's asking each of the following questions, a man or woman.

- "Can we talk?"
- "Hey, want to fool around?"

As you probably guessed, the first speaker is female, the second male. In part this difference in how men and women ask for intimacy stems from how each tends to experience sexual arousal. A man who is more visually oriented than a woman experiences desire first, arousal second. For a woman it's often the opposite.

She's aroused first and then feels a desire for sexuality. This is one of the reasons why women prefer longer periods of foreplay before intercourse. When a man arouses his partner through stroking, kissing, and exchanging loving words, this foreplay often leads her to an experience of a deep desire that may not have been present when he initially approached her.

Loving talk between partners is different than the problem solving type of communication that must go on during weekly check-ins. Neither is like the light banter you may exchange in the course of a day. In fact, it's imperative to keep your sexuality free of "real life" talk as much as possible. Instead, you should make sexuality a sacred time and place where your only agenda is to make room for expressions of love and laughter that stem from the joy of profound connecting. No discussions about money, the kids, problems with a friend or relative, or knocks at the door or phone calls should intrude.

The Challenge of the Familiar

There is a basic assumption and a paradox in most married sexuality. First, that true love means each partner will find the other "enough" to satisfy his sexual needs for the duration of the marriage. In other words, despite the constant and nearly equal incidence of infidelity among married men and women, most couples believe they are signing up for monogamy when they marry. Operating on this assumption, they either adjust behavior to look but not indulge in sex outside of marriage or they cheat. From this assumption also comes the paradox: that with familiarity the original sexual attraction that drew the two of you together can fade rapidly. What is any married couple to do?

First, it helps to acknowledge the obvious. You are not the first and will not be the last couple to face this situation. When you're dating, and before you live together as a couple, it's easy to look your best on date night, to keep your nasty moods outside of your partner's presence, and to arrange time to be alone without asking anyone's permission. This all changes with marriage and a loss of sexual excitement is often its collateral damage. However, if the feelings accompanying these dynamics—resentment, fear, jealousy, boredom—were to be discussed honestly and frequently with your partner, there is no doubt that the damage can be minimized.

 Fact

Sex means different things and functions differently for men and women. According to John Gray in *Mars and Venus in the Bedroom*, "It is sex that allows a man to feel his need for love, while it is receiving love that helps a woman to feel her hunger for sex."

The Frequency Debate

The main issue a therapist confronts when discussing sexuality in marriage concerns is the frequency of sex. In his therapy practice, Stephen Martin has asked thousands of couples this question, "If you could have it your way, how often would you and your partner have sex?" In his clients' answers, he finds that the majority of men say once or twice a day, while the majority of women say once a week. Herein he says lies the potential problem, unless the issue of frequency of sex is discussed and a compromise found.

Monogamy Brings Responsibility

Often the issue of monogamy in marriage is discussed in a vacuum. One or both attest to their desire for monogamy, but the conversation doesn't include an honest examination of the primary sexual relationship between the two partners. Is it not relevant to include the fact that one partner is withholding sex if the other partner is being judged for going elsewhere to meet his sexual needs? "With monogamy comes responsibility" means that if you want your partner to be monogamous, you have to be willing to participate in a sexual relationship. One husband in marriage therapy once expressed his feelings this way: "My wife expects because she is not hungry, that I should not eat." He has a good point: Simply saying "no" cannot be the end of the conversation about sex in a marriage.

E ssential

Compromise is still the best route to marital happiness. As Dr. Deborah Newman wrote in *Then God Created Woman*, "In every marriage, someone is having sex more often than he or she wants, and someone is having sex less than he or she would like. In good marriages, couples compromise and are able to give and receive in order to satisfy both partners."

Once sexuality is dormant in a relationship, the problem needs to be addressed from several perspectives. One route to a solution is through communication. The woman and man need to express needs and desires, and eventually within a monogamous relationship, compromise must be found so both feel satisfied with the sexual union. While lack of sex is never the sole reason for the end of a marriage, a lack of intimacy—including having sex—can derail the best relationships if not attended to.

Here is one couple's experience with these delicate issues.

Jim and Susan were in their early forties and hadn't had sexual relations in over two years when they first came for marriage therapy. After the birth of their second child, Susan couldn't lose the thirty pounds she'd gained during her pregnancy. Meanwhile Jim felt frustrated, lonely, and unloved. The strain of his wanting sex and her repeatedly saying "No" had taken its toll on the relationship. He rarely asked anymore. "But he didn't have to," Susan said, "it's always in the background." On weekends, the two dealt with the household and kids, rarely doing anything alone as a couple.

"The problem is I don't feel sexy," Susan said after Jim shared his feelings.

"But I still think you're sexy," he said. "Isn't that enough?" Susan looked away as tears started to fall down her cheeks. "You're just saying that," she said. Clearly it was not enough.

Jim and Susan still loved each other and wanted to stay together, and they were way too young to give up sex. What could they do?

It's important for a couple like Jim and Susan to know that their situation is a common one. Many wives who no longer like their bodies refuse to believe their husbands still want them sexually. As a result, a woman in Susan's spot takes her anger and mistrust out on her man. It's a dangerous point in a marriage, one that can lead to a husband having affairs, or it can cause the couple to become permanently estranged.

First, they both had to recognize and accept what was actually happening in the relationship. In the language of self-growth, they had to "accept what is." Then, each had to both come to a clear decision to fix what was wrong. Clearly, Susan had not yet done either of these things.

To help his wife move past her insecurity about whether she was still sexually desirable to him, Jim would have to convince Susan that he found her attractive; essentially, he had to woo her back enlisting the same feelings and using the methods he'd employed to win her love in the beginning of their relationship.

Ultimately, for their relationship to thrive, Susan had to decide whether or not to lose the weight for herself, not for Jim. At the same time, if she expected Jim to remain faithful in the marriage, Susan had a responsibility to continue their sexual relationship. With honest communication, and several weeks of working at creating romance, time alone, and playing with (non-goal-oriented) sensual touch, Jim and Susan slowly rekindled their emotional and sexual connection and resumed a satisfying sex life.

A good sexual relationship takes a real commitment to the relationship, a willingness to move through uncomfortable feelings, and good old-fashioned effort. Part of this effort involves a reclaiming of some of the feelings that each of you experienced during your initial courtship. Not to go back in time, but to enrich the present with some of the adoration that enchants the early stages of the love relationship but falls away as everyday life takes hold.

Romancing the Marriage

Romance has gotten a bad rap. As the opening chapter of this book stated, falling in love is not a good enough foundation for marriage. The problem is that couples and therapists alike may have thrown the baby out with the bath water, leaving an insufficient role for romance in marriage. A little romantic feeling goes a long way when communication falters and hearts shut down. Said another way, giving and receiving expressions of love and adoration is an effective antidote to the tendency in long-term relationship to take each other for granted. One antidote for relationship boredom is to bring back some old-time romance.

Part of the problem for many couples for whom romance feels like ancient history is the crass commercialization of its rituals.

 **Alert**

A man dreads Valentine's Day in inverse proportion to the degree a woman loves it. The problem with hearts and flowers from a male perspective is the typical man's resistance and (for some) hostility at being told exactly when and how he's supposed to show his adoration for the woman in his life.

It's not that deep down men don't like to be romantic; in fact, men do. He just hates being told to show up with flowers or jewelry in lockstep with the rest of his gender. It generally works better for a man when he can individually decide how to reclaim romance in his own way, and then act with authenticity from his heart. What's in romance for a man? He gets an emotionally and sexually vulnerable partner who's ready to receive his love and return it in kind. From a male perspective, this can be plenty reward for such a small effort in the romance department.

Really, What Is Romance?

In medieval times, a love of God and of the beloved woman was combined in the chivalric tradition of romantic poetry. At their essence the songs of these troubadours were expressions of a man's adoration for the woman he loved from afar, the distance being due to the fact that she was often married or otherwise unavailable to him. He loved her for her purity, her beauty, and for the devotional feelings she inspired in him even if he couldn't have her to himself, and this represented an ideal of love, which in many ways was closer to a spiritual love than romantic love as we think of it today.

While chaste love is not the goal of modern marital love, this idealized romantic tradition in Western civilization can serve to make modern love a fuller, more integrated experience of heart, spirit, and flesh. The declarations of love and adoration made by these medieval knights were nonmaterial gifts to the beloved, whether displays of words or actions. This is the chivalric tradition encapsulated by the image of a knight laying down his life for the fair lady who inspired all that was good in him. In Eastern religions and also in Jungian psychological terms, the knight and the fair lady are viewed as two parts of the same person. These aspects of the self are the feminine receptive and relational or yin, complemented by the masculine active or yang principle. Both are necessary, and it is through the union of opposites that balance is reached, both within an individual and in a marriage. This is the essence of the healing power of sexuality when honesty, love, commitment, and respect for the other are all present in the relationship.

Say What You Love about Her

A simple exercise that can help you both get back in touch with your feelings of romance that may have gotten lost in the course of living your daily lives is to look deep into your heart and come up with a list of thirty things you love about your partner. You can write these down on a special greeting card or on a plain piece of paper. When completed, hand your list to him with a single red rose or put it inside a box of chocolates. The idea is to make it a simple, but very special, romantic gesture.

E ssential

As a way to enhance your own words, consider drawing on some of the most romantic love poems ever written. Get thee to the library and look for Lord Byron, Percy Shelley, Emily Dickinson, Rumi, or John Keats. Then check out the modern poets like Rainer Maria Rilke, William Carlos Williams, or e. e. cummings. These word masters can help transform you into the romantic you once were.

Here are some of the loving things spouses say to each other while doing this exercise. As you compile your own list, keep in mind that each sentence starts with these words: "What I love the most about you is. . . ."

- You have the best laugh of anyone I know
- The twinkle in your eyes when you think I look sexy
- The way you spoon with me at night
- Your voice, especially when you sing in church
- Your naked body
- Your homemade pasta and sauce
- The way you keep your eyes open when we make love
- The way you always know when I reach orgasm

And so on. Maybe one of these applies to your feelings about your partner. Pick any that ring true and add others that are unique to you and your beloved. Every relationship is different, and there are reasons why the two of you work well as a couple. The point of this exercise is to remember those reasons. Once you get started, hopefully you won't be able to stop. And that's the idea of this exercise. You're going to recover the adoration that's lying within you but perhaps has lain silent for too long.

Sex by Appointment

At first glance, planning ahead and writing down in your date book the date and time for future sexual encounters with your partner might appear at odds with romance. It can actually be a sign of a vibrant sex life. By arranging for privacy, perhaps by booking a baby-sitter and leaving the house or sending the kids to Grandma's, and by choosing the leisure time to enjoy each other without other pressing obligations or exhaustion, you are honoring the sexual intimacy you value and wish to preserve in your relationship.

At a minimum, every couple should make the effort to spend alone-time together solely for the purpose of sensual or sexual intimacy every week. Ideally this is an unbreakable "date" when you can have real privacy, but if this is just not possible, a compromise should be made to do it every other week, but nothing less than this is advisable. With sexuality, as in many other aspects of life, 90 percent of success is simply "showing up." When you both commit to making sexuality a priority, you're making a crucial statement to each other. This simple act opens up the space for trust, both within your sexuality and in the larger relationship.

Pregnancy, Nursing, and Married Sex

A rude awakening for many new fathers is the feeling of being replaced in a wife's heart, mind, and bosom by the new baby. Even those fathers who think they're prepared for this experience can find it disconcerting. Feelings of abandonment and even sadness are not unusual. The most important thing to know is that these are entirely normal and, in most cases, temporary experiences and feelings. The truth of the matter is that the new mother falls in love with her new-born baby. This is entirely as nature intended, and how it must be if the mother and child are to bond normally.

If it's a first child and if the woman is nursing her infant, the experience of one-on-one bonding can be even more intense and potentially alienating for a new father. As a man, the most important thing for you to do is to take a step back and appreciate the beauty of this picture of maternal love. Then you can and should partici-pate in the bonding process as a father to your newborn by holding, cooing, singing, and doing all the things that new parents do when expressing the astonishingly deep feelings of love they have for a newborn child. It's not exactly the same as what a new mother expe-riences, but it's similarly enriching. It also gives you some emotional sustenance for what is often an arduous and sleepless time without much in the way of physical contact with your wife whose body is frankly committed elsewhere.

 **Alert**

A woman's interest in returning to sex with her partner returns anywhere from six months to two years after she gives birth—rarely before. But, if a woman remains sexually shut down to her husband for longer than six months, it may be necessary to get some couples counseling to help the two of you make the transi-tion from being just two to now three.

The transition from a couple to a family with a newborn can be rocky—both physically and emotionally—for both partners. Exhaus-tion is a real factor. Some women will feel torn between the needs of the child and those of her husband. Her own needs are often pushed out of sight. The best solution for all concerned is time. One of the biggest mistakes young couples make is allowing their sexuality to dwindle after the arrival of children. It's very easy to justify doing so when children require so much time and energy. Don't let it happen. If you do, it will negatively affect your children as family is built upon the strength of your marriage. This is the most critical time to stick to a weekly or biweekly date night to be alone and intimate, although it can also be the hardest time to do it. If intercourse is still physically painful for the woman, or if exhaustion makes her desire go AWOL, it's still important to touch, cuddle, and share intimate feelings as a couple. Giving her a massage is likely to be received as a heavenly gift.

Keeping Sex New as Your Marriage Matures

Beyond the pressures of parenthood and the reality of physical exhaustion for today's busy couples, there is a challenge in simply keeping your sexuality alive during the years of a long-term marriage. In Chapter 9, this subject is gone into more thoroughly with plenty of suggestions and exercises to help. Suffice to say here that your sexuality must change as you and your partner change.

You are no longer the ingénue and he's no longer the young stud you married, but this is not the main problem that keeps married sex from remaining vibrant and alive. On the contrary, your greater trust as a couple and your individual maturation into a more sensitive man or woman open up new possibilities for sexual expression between you. The challenge is to keep exploring these new avenues for sexual intimacy, to let your imaginations take you into unexplored fantasies, and to let your closeness bring you into even more profound reaches of sacred connection.

Chapter 9

Bringing Passion Back

IF, AS RESEARCHERS say, romance fades for most couples within six to nine months of their wedding day, how are you supposed to maintain a satisfying sex life for the years and decades you hope to spend with your spouse? Forget about ignoring the problem; untreated problems only get worse. Nor should you expect to find marital happiness by becoming celibate buddies with your spouse, essentially shutting down your sexuality. Unless two parties agree to a cessation of sexual relations for health or another mutually acceptable reason, leaving sensuality or sexuality out of the marriage can leave one partner bitter and the relationship weaker.

Let's Talk about Sex

What are the other typical fixes offered by friends or so-called relationship experts? While diverting your sexual needs to an affair with someone else will undoubtedly produce short-term drama to heat up a marriage, it is not a long-term solution. An affair, discovered or not, can also aggravate feelings of abandonment or distrust, feelings that may be present already if your sexuality is absent or minimally present. Finally, contrary to the views of many, simply adding variety or novelty will not rescue a dying sexual relationship. Buying sexy lingerie and sex toys, trying new sexual positions, or even swinging with another couple can provide diversion and fleeting relief for sexual doldrums, but it can also produce more tension between partners, especially if one feels pressured by the other.

So, while any or all of these things can spice up the relationship if the two partners are on the same page and both wish to try something new, these novel behaviors will not substitute for the one essential step you must take if you wish to bring passion back to your relationship—that is, restoring and deepening the connection between the two of you.

Your connection must first be emotional, and for an emotional relationship to grow it must be nurtured by positive communication, expressions of appreciation, and a willingness to deal with the hard issues. A woman must feel safe and adored to be open sexually. A man must feel appreciated to be satisfied in sex and marriage. If you can nurture these feelings throughout the years you're together, you'll have a good foundation for healthy sexuality in your marriage.

For many couples, a deep connection that can sustain marriage for the long term also requires the presence of something larger than the two of you. Whether that greater thing is God or a higher power, a strong sense of community, or a devotion to serving others, passion in marriage thrives on an exchange of energy between two people that is rooted in what many call the divine.

Deepening Your Connection

What does sex have to do with spirituality and how does a connection to the divine translate into a richer sexual relationship? Sexual pleasure is one of the primary joys of being human, but it is much more than a pleasurable physical experience. In addition to the possibility of creating new life, sexuality represents the joining of two people on the most essential level of their being. Contrary to the early teachings of Christian theologians St. Augustine and St. Paul before him, the direct experience of many people over the millennia suggests that the coming together of powerful energies in sexual intercourse makes it a sacred, creative act—with or without procreation as the couple's intent.

By joining your most vulnerable self with the one you love in sacred sexuality you have the potential to give and receive human love at its most profound and productive level. As a result of this deep emotional and spiritual connection, you become a more loving, more giving, and more fulfilled person—alone and together. Using the scientific method and plain common sense, it's plain to see that sexually satisfied people are healthier and happier. A sexually fulfilled woman beams her happiness to anyone she encounters. A sexually fulfilled man greets his day with unrivaled enthusiasm.

 Fact

Tantric teachings about sex prescribe practices intended to increase orgasmic potential and enhance the couple's intimate connection. The basic techniques encourage lovers to maintain eye contact, delay his orgasm, increase her arousal, share breath while kissing, and try a variety of ancient sexual positions. There are many books on tantric sex that explain and demonstrate these practices in detail.

Ancient Sexual Wisdom

Although the Christian religion historically equated sexuality and sin, several Eastern spiritual traditions (and many modern Western, Christian teachings) hold human sexuality as an aspect of the divine. Indian Tantrism and Chinese Taoism are centuries-old spiritual disciplines that integrate enlightened sexuality and spirituality as two compatible paths to a happy life and spiritual fulfillment. These traditions teach that certain conscious sexual practices permit the exchange of male (yang) and female (yin) energy. This exchange, the traditions say, is essential to meaning and balance in life and relationship. Many Western couples have discovered tantric sexuality as a way to deepen their marital connection and support each partner's spiritual growth.

Your Sex Story

Healthy sexual intimacy can be a critical healing tool for couples. However, when someone who was raised to believe his sexuality was sinful confronts sexual problems in his marriage, feelings of shame instilled early in his life can interfere with resolving sexual problems in the present—even ruining a marriage in the process. Just as you constructed the story of your relationship with money in Chapter 6, it's important to understand your sexual history, beginning in childhood. Were you taught that sexual desire outside of procreation is sinful? If the answer is yes, you are not unusual in Western culture.

Far too often, youngsters are not taught that sexuality is an important, healthy aspect of personal and spiritual growth or of a relationship. The reason for this often is that parents want children to wait to become sexual until they're emotionally mature enough to handle the powerful urges involved. So, they attempt to create a negative aura around sex, putting a taboo on all things sexual, with the result that parents achieve the exact opposite of what they intended.

Here are some statements to complete to help you put together the story of your early learning about and experiences with sexuality:

- My mother taught me that sex is . . .
- My father taught me that sex is . . .
- My first feeling of being sexually attractive to the opposite came when . . .
- My first sexual experience was . . .
- The aftermath of that experience made me feel . . .
- My religious upbringing taught me that sex is . . .
- My own belief about the importance of sex is . . .
- I feel most sexually alive today when . . .
- I am happy/not happy with my body today . . .
- My partner makes me feel sexy when . . .
- The last time I really enjoyed sex was . . .

Without healthy sexuality, many marriages do not endure difficult times. Sex in marriage is a double-edged sword. Left abandoned or unsatisfying, sex can doom a marriage. If kept alive or re-enlivened, sex can make marriage blossom and bring fulfillment to both partners.

You Can Relight the Flame

The most common dynamic that therapists see in marriages when a couple is not experiencing a happy sex life is a sexually frustrated husband with a sexually resistant wife. This is not to say the roles sometimes aren't reversed, but the first scenario is much more likely to be the case. Maybe one or both of you are overworked and not getting enough sleep. Perhaps there are young children. There are plenty of understandable reasons why it may be happening. To get from a sexual standoff to a newly revitalized sex life first requires an acknowledgment of what is going on, and then a shared intention to change the situation into something more satisfying for both partners.

The Talk

Many couples avoid it at all costs. They would rather spend the entire weekend immersed in chores, shopping, or carting the kids from place to place. They'd prefer to complain about the lack of sex in their marriage with their respective same-sex friends, even make jokes about it. They'll do anything but have a conversation with a spouse that might address what's missing in their sexuality. Why all this avoidance? Guilt, shame, and fear, among other things. Fear that by opening the Pandora's Box of sexual dissatisfaction, he might get a rude surprise, perhaps have to listen to other complaints about how he's failing her. Or, she dreads hearing how cold and sexually unresponsive she is . . . when in reality she misses the physical affection she used to receive from him as much as he does.

There are two major things missing from a marriage stuck in this stalemate: sexuality and communication. In their place you'll find suppressed anger, hurt, and fear. Depending on how long the stalemate between the two has been in effect, there are also poor habits reflecting the physical and emotional distance between them, which has become the new status quo.

From the outside, this couple will appear to be bored in the marriage. They'll snap at each other and offer frequent criticisms. Very often in this tense standoff one partner will throw a grenade by having an extramarital affair. Although some may think this turn of events signals the end of the marriage, often it means the opposite: That the partners have grown tired of their stalemate and wish to begin the process of healing the marriage.

Start Inside

Whoever once said "Happiness is an inside job" had it exactly right. It's hard to feel sexually attracted to your partner if you are not feeling physically fit or content in your own body. The issue goes far beyond attractiveness. A poor self-image is the "elephant in the room" in many dysfunctional relationships. Too many marriages, and even marriage therapists, regard self-image as an off-limits topic for discussion or confrontation when attempting to deal with dysfunction in a sexual relationship. Whether you're attempting to bring sexuality back with the help of a therapist or you're doing it on your own, the place to start is within yourself. One way to kick-start the process is to do take some steps to gently wake up your senses, beginning with you, alone. Take the time to romance yourself. Some simple exercises that will help include:

- **Body relaxation.** Sit or lie down on the floor or the bed. Put your attention one by one on every part of your body, commanding each to relax completely. Go from your head to your toes, taking ten or fifteen minutes to release all your tension. Count from ten to zero, for your forehead, neck, arms, pelvis, and so on until each is completely relaxed.
- **A long, hot soak.** Do the relaxation exercise above, then visualize yourself back in a warm fluid womb and rest there.
- **Move.** Take a daily walk, a run up the stairs, or dance to your favorite music

- **Use positive affirmations**. "I am a beautiful, zesty, sexy woman . . ." "I am a strong, virile man. . . ."
- **Rediscover sexual self-pleasuring.** Try a vibrator, get a mirror, and lock the door
- **Sensualize your environment.** Light candles, get a fur rug or a new duvet, hang nudes on the walls, move the stereo into the bedroom

Starting Fresh by Making Time and Effort

There is a lot that one person can do to reawaken sensually and sexually, but, ultimately, reviving sexuality in a marriage requires the participation of both partners. If you are the one asking for your partner's involvement in a sexual renewal, be sure to frame your request positively. "I'd like to put more effort in making our sex life better," sounds sweeter and a lot more inviting than "Our sex is so boring, I can't stand it anymore." Certainly threats and ultimatums are not constructive. Be sure to begin gently, perhaps offer to do something for him—give a massage or foot rub, for example.

If your partner responds either tentatively or negatively, try not to over react. You may have caught him by surprise. He may still feel stuck in the old stalemate. Give him time to process your request. Be positive. Before you interpret your partner's lack of enthusiasm as being a message about you, or your body, consider these questions:

- Is he overtired and stressed out?
- Has he recently experienced a loss?
- Is he just getting over a physical illness?
- Is he worried about his work? Or is he insecure about his job being there?

Finally, let him know that your offer stands even if he's not ready to take you up on it just then. Then he can come back to you when he's ready. If he responds enthusiastically, allow things to unfold without pushing or intellectualizing. After enjoying some sensual time together, you may wish to take the opportunity to open up the conversation. If this feels like it would help the two of you open up further to clear the air, then by all means speak about what's been going on between the two of you sexually.

Remember, you're looking to share feelings at this time, not to assign blame or offer a negative prognosis on the past or future of your sexuality. The most important thing you can express to him is your real desire to bring back the sexual passion you used to enjoy in your relationship. When you talk, keep touching him. It's amazing how much love can be expressed in a simple stroke.

Go Slow!

Ironically, the best way sex therapists have found to help people rejuvenate sexuality is by advising the couple to do anything but have sexual intercourse for some period of time. The idea is to take all pressure off and keep performance completely off the table. Sensuality comes before sexuality. Playful touching, kissing, and caressing are what will ideally unfold at this stage. There's also some counter-suggestion going on here; no matter how old people are, they tend to rebel against something they're told to do.

So, whether you take all the advice or a part, your objective is to go slow. Envision what might happen if you were to go back to your very first date, before you ever shared a single passionate kiss. Try to recapture the initial feelings and small steps you took before you both "opted in" to full sexual expression. What did his kisses feel like? What about the first electric spark you exchanged? When and where did it happen?

Massage for Lovers

Massage can be done as a sumptuous three-course dinner or as a brief snack—a small loving gesture at the end of a long day. When you don't have enough time or energy for a complete body massage, a hand or foot massage is a great gift. Or it can be a part of the pre-amble before sexual activity. You'll be surprised how much energy comes to you once you get in a flow doing the massage on your partner.

Even if neither of you has been trained in massage techniques, you can help relax tense muscles and give your partner the gift of loving touch. Every part of the body responds to the stimulus of touch. One thinks immediately of a lover's breasts, genitals, and lips. But what about her toes, earlobes, stomach, ankles, and forehead? Each of these parts of the body should receive loving attention during a massage.

The Relaxation Massage

1. Choose a quiet, private place, such as a bedroom, or the living room when you can have it to yourselves. Drape the bed, floor, or massage table with a sheet.
2. Light some candles; doing so will immediately change the mood. Put on some relaxing music at a low volume.
3. Warm up the room with the heat on.
4. The woman (or man) receiving the massage gets nude, lies down on her back, and begins to concentrate on her breathing, inhaling for a few seconds and then letting her breath float out.
5. The man (or woman) giving the massage takes a small amount (a few drops) of scented massage oil (olive oil works fine) and warms it up in the palms of his hands.
6. The man then centers himself by putting his attention on his own breathing. He places his hands on her shoulders to make an energy connection between the two of them, letting their breathing get in sync.
7. The woman turns over onto her stomach and continues slow deep breathing.
8. The man places his oiled palms on the small of her back. He rubs her back using both whole hands in gentle, long strokes. He strokes from the base of the back, up toward the neck, and then back down the sides of the back. He does this for at least two minutes.
9. The woman puts her attention to whatever part of her body is being stroked. The massage is usually done in silence

so each person can remain in his body, feeling the energy going out and coming in.

10. The man gradually increases his pressure as he massages her back and each subsequent area. He kneads the flesh around her shoulders and neck, common places for tension. He follows her muscles across the shoulders and down each arm.

11. Returning to the small of her back, he uses both hands to rub the flesh away from the spine and then back toward it, keeping in rhythm.

12. At base of the spine, he begins stroking downward across the buttocks; then sweeps his hands down each leg several times using a lighter motion.

13. He strokes her calves, paying particular attention to her feet, rubbing beneath the arch, pulling gently on the toes.

14. When he has finished the massage, her turns the receiver back over and gently pulls the sheet up to cover her, in order to hold in her body warmth. She may fall asleep, or she can rest for a while and then reciprocate by massaging him.

There's a very good chance that even a relaxation massage can serve to arouse a lover sexually, particularly when the time, setting, and mood are right. If that is your intent, you can make your strokes and movements linger longer and closer to the recipient's erogenous zones: the upper thighs, stomach, groin, breasts, and lips. Make your movements long and slow. As you do, make your touch lighter, almost teasing. Your goal now is not to apply pressure as much as it is to build erotic tension. Essentially, you're teasing her, and both of you can enjoy the playfulness of the experience. Whether you have intercourse at this point is entirely up to the two of you.

Role-Playing and Fantasy Games

Everyone has fantasies, even if you don't think you do. They happen while you dream at night or sit (daydreaming) in your cubicle during the day. Men and women have them, albeit usually different kinds. Some sexual fantasies feature erotic situations and scenes you might like to act out with your partner. Others remain strictly fantasies, meaning you wouldn't want them to occur anytime, anywhere outside of the privacy of your imagination.

However, this latter category may include fantasies you may wish to share, meaning *tell* your sexual partner. Indeed, many fantasies, too hot for real life, can add a zesty erotic edge to a couple's lovemaking when verbalized in the heat of passion. Using fantasies and role-playing to enliven sexuality can be effective as long as each partner is equally comfortable with the process and is game to play with the particular characters, actions, props, and places the other wishes to try out.

 **Alert**

> Lovers who wish to try out fantasies involving force or gentle restraints should choose a safe word before they begin. This is a word (it should never be "no" or "stop"), which unequivocally means, "Stop immediately." A safe word like "pineapple" or "computer" leaves no room for confusion about one partner's intent to stop or take a break from your sex play. A safe word allows both of you to let go and enjoy the fantasy.

A very common female sex fantasy, perhaps the most common, is where a man "takes" his woman, essentially requiring her to submit to his greater strength or commanding words. This only works if both partners have agreed to it beforehand, but the fact is that both men and women enjoy playing out this fantasy. Many women, especially powerful ones, say they like letting go of control in the bedroom, either occasionally or frequently. Many a man who is quite comfortable sharing power with women in the workplace, or splitting duties with a wife at home, relishes the idea of playing the brave and daring hero of his boyhood dreams. One way for both to try on these roles, or experiment, is by playing out the fantasies in sex play. Many couples like to use costumes to play priests, maids, courtesans, pirates, and cops; they may use props, including handcuffs, ropes, and masks, to enact full scenes, either scripted or spontaneous.

The Blind Date

This exercise is essentially a role-play and a date night put together. Your goal is to go back in time and enact a first meeting between the two of you in a slightly risqué setting, perhaps happy hour in a bar or at a train station. The idea is to spot each other across the room or platform, and go through the paces of seduction—complete with pick-up lines, sexy banter, and outrageous flirting. The key is to make it very different from your usual night out routine. In other words, don't go to your favorite restaurant or someplace you might encounter someone who knows you. The goal is to make the familiar unfamiliar again, adding an element of risk and rediscovering the chemistry that originally brought you together.

Give Completely for Eight Hours

This activity may seem simple, but it's not. As an exercise in submission, it can be very powerful and transforming if you give yourself over to it. By spending one whole day serving your lover, and likewise being served, you'll discover new aspects of yourself and your partner. Through this experience, both of you can create a new emotional space for giving and taking within the relationship, with a potentially powerful and positive impact on your sex life.

Here's the surprising part of this exercise. Whereas you might at first think it's harder to serve than to be served, the opposite is often true. It can be difficult to ask for things, and receive exactly what say you want, regardless of how silly or self-indulgent the request feels, hour after hour. Why is it so hard? For one thing, it's challenging for many people to know and ask for what they actually want. Then, you must get past feeling selfish or bossy. For many adults, especially self-reliant, independent types, none of this is easy.

For the one giving, your challenge is to feel selfless. This means putting aside any resentment you might have about who's been doing what housework or childcare in your real lives. What you'll find when you perform service for each other is that you'll eventually move past these inhibitions. You'll discover you really enjoy giving to your partner and in turn relish receiving from him—when it's acknowledged.

Acknowledgment is key, and it's often a revelation to couples how far a little appreciation can go toward creating harmony in a relationship. When you've completed your days of service, you can share your internal experiences with each other. Of all the things your partner did or asked for, what meant the most to you? What service gave you less of a thrill than you might have thought? Hint: If you allow it to, this exercise can produce positive repercussions in the bedroom, where honest and unrestrained giving and receiving are essential parts of healthy sexuality.

E ssential

There will be many ups and downs in this relationship, and as Mrs. Anterbus put it in Thorton Wilder's play, "The Skin of Our Teeth,": "I didn't marry you because you were perfect. I married you because you gave me a promise. This promise made up for your faults, and the promise I made to you made up for mine."

Renewing Your Sexual Relationship for the Long Term

After rescuing a dormant sex life you will learn that you and your partner have gained a whole new set of cognitive and hands-on skills that can be used again—whenever the need arises. The other thing to take away from this chapter is the certainty that the need for sexual renewal will arise again. Marriage is a work in progress, never static. If it's standing still, that's a danger sign. Each of you matures by going through crises and happy milestones or life passages that will change you, and by extension the marriage.

If you make it as a couple, you will be very different people at the middle and end points of your marriage than you were at the start. If you stay together, it's highly likely you've mastered the art of keeping sexuality alive in whatever ways work for the two of you. Know one thing, as your bodies and minds change, the children come and go, and careers wax and wane, all the ways that work to keep sexuality alive for your relationship will change too.

The only difference from here on is that if you hit another bump in the road, and it starts to feel like the end of your marriage, you might recognize the situation or conflict as another possible new beginning. The wise couple knows when to fight for their relationship and when to capitulate. Be sure to take a good look at what's happening between the two of you, and then turn your gaze inside: Is this crisis an opportunity to alter your own thinking or behavior, to give more, to let go of an old hurt, or to renew your relationship? More often than not, the answer is yes!

Chapter 10

Surviving Infidelity

INFIDELITY IS AN extremely difficult issue for couples, but numerous studies show most get past one partner's affair and stay married. Approximately one marriage in five where there's been an episode of infidelity comes to an end as a direct result of the extramarital affair. For some, the crisis that erupts after the discovery of an affair becomes an opportunity for the renewal of commitment between husband and wife. This is most likely the case when the affair becomes the catalyst for marriage therapy, where underlying issues can be brought out into the open and addressed.

Defining Infidelity

Infidelity has a variety of definitions, depending on the couple or individual. For most people, marital cheating is strictly defined as one partner having sexual relations—viewed as sexual intercourse and/or oral sex—with a third party. For some, infidelity also applies to nonsexual situations, for example, when a married man forms a deep emotional bond with a woman to whom he is not married, or when a married woman flirts or enjoys personal conversations with a male coworker. Yet there are married men and women who give their partners a wide berth to form close friendships with members of the opposite sex, as long as the interactions remain hands off.

However you define infidelity, when it occurs (that is, when your partner violates your expectations about what is appropriate in relationship to others) you will most likely feel betrayed. This is true whether or not you ever sat down as a couple to discuss and define what each of you means by cheating. Having this conversation is an important conversation to have early on in any marriage, and it's the only way you'll be able to arrive at common definitions and expectations. Here are some considerations to assist you in this process.

Essential

In the American Sexual Survey conducted by The National Opinion Research Center at The University of Chicago, researchers found that 22 percent of married men and 15 percent of married women had had at least one extramarital affair. According to this survey of ten thousand married people conducted over twenty years, most cheating happens three to five years into a marriage by a man dissatisfied with sex, or by a woman who feels emotionally deprived in her marriage.

Looking Is Not the Same as Doing

Men, especially, like the idea (if not the reality) of variety when it comes to the opposite sex. This is perhaps the greatest nonsecret about the male of the species, and yet many a woman takes it as a personal affront when a man's eyes stray away from where she's sitting to follow an attractive woman walking by in a short skirt. Then there's the reality that some men and women, usually extroverts or more socially outgoing types, have more flirtatious personalities than others. For whatever reason, extroverts are frequently attracted to their opposites, and thus end up marrying more introverted or reserved spouses.

The following behaviors may be black and white to both of you, or, conversely, they may fall into a gray area somewhere between okay and not okay. Which of these behaviors is infidelity to you?

- Playful flirting, touching
- Giving intimate gifts to another
- Sexually suggestive talk
- Sharing deep, private thoughts and feelings with another
- Becoming "best friends" with someone of the opposite sex
- Kissing another person on the lips
- Developing a crush on someone else
- Exchanging personal e-mails or text messages
- Engaging in specific types of contact (such as sleeping in the same bed)
- Having sexually suggestive online chats or virtual affairs

 Fact

The American Sexual Survey researchers found that 15 percent of married men and 7 percent of married women had engaged in online sex, while 66 percent of those polled said they considered this behavior cheating. Twenty percent of those polled had romantically kissed someone other than a spouse, which 83 percent defined as cheating.

Coming to a definition of cheating is impossible if couples won't discuss their expectations for fidelity. Some may consciously or unconsciously avoid defining what constitutes cheating since, by keeping the ground rules unclear, they may believe it makes it easier for them to cheat. If you don't know what the rules are, you really can't break them—at least that's what may be in the back of one partner's mind.

Why Men and Women Cheat

Even if you put aside the question of whether (or not) monogamy is a natural state for human beings, anywhere from 30 to 60 percent of married partners (depending on the study) who promise fidelity to a spouse admit to doing the opposite (at some point in their married lives). Researchers say that the average length of an affair is less than one week, but the result is often weeks, months, or years of emotional trauma and conflict for the marriage. Trust is very hard to re-establish once it's lost. So why do people risk all that they hold dear for a short-term thrill?

Essential

Some couples, but not all, view emotional infidelity—where a spouse develops a close friendship with another member of the opposite sex—as a serious threat to their marriage. Those couples who hold this view see emotional intimacy as a likely precursor to sexual infidelity, and so they believe it should be avoided. If the emotional liaison has already occurred, they want it confessed to and stopped.

He Cheats

Every study on the subject of marital infidelity shows that a married man cheats only somewhat more often than a married woman—he just does it differently. A man tends to go outside his marriage because he wants more sex or more sexual variety. Men have more one-night stands than women, and they seem to have an easier time separating infidelity from whatever problems they face at home. They are more likely to have several extramarital affairs whereas women tend to stray once. Men also tend to have briefer liaisons. However, according to psychologist William F. Harley, author of *His Needs, Her Needs*, if a man forms a long-term extramarital attachment, he will often find it harder (than a woman in the same situation) to let go of the other person—even if the relationship with his wife improves.

She Cheats

A woman who goes outside her marriage is far more likely than a straying man to be searching for emotional attention, or reassurance of her desirability to the opposite sex. A woman is also more likely to fall in love with the man with whom she has an affair and more frequently considers leaving her marriage because of an affair. When women cheat, they tend to view the infidelity as a symptom of deeper problems in their marriage. However, again according to William Harley, if a woman's marriage improves, meaning her husband begins to provide the emotional sustenance she went outside the marriage to find, she has an easier time letting go of her outside lover and returning her full attention to the marriage.

 Fact

Research shows that only 20 to 27 percent of divorces are attributable to an extramarital affair. The more common reason given is "growing apart emotionally" and when one "did not feel loved or appreciated."

They Cheat

Although there are differences between men and women's conduct of and reasons for having extramarital affairs, there are also some significant similarities. Interestingly, the majority of men and women who admitted to cheating believed their behavior to be morally wrong, although more men rationalized their behavior saying their wives had stopped wanting sex. Both men and women are capable of using cheating as a form of revenge—for instance, he gets back at her for having an affair by initiating his own. As to where most affairs originate, with so many more men and women now working side by side, it probably comes as no surprise that office romances have become the most common type of extramarital affairs.

The Confrontation

Although the American Sex Survey reported that the spouse who stays behind finds out about only 2 to 3 percent of a husband or wife's extramarital affairs, when one is discovered, a confrontation is most often the result. What follows is the story of Scott and Diane, a couple Stephen Martin saw in marriage therapy to deal with an episode of infidelity. The dynamics involved are very typical of the aftermath of one partner's discovery of the other's affair.

> *"She had sex with him in our bed while I was at work!"*
>
> *Scott could barely contain his rage as he described the particulars of his wife's betrayal during our initial phone call. At a pause, I asked him how he found out about Diane's affair with this other man.*
>
> *"I hacked into her e-mail," Scott answered.*
>
> *Where upon Scott discovered that Alan lived in Atlanta, which is where he'd met Diane at a computer software conference. Over six months, they conducted their clandestine romance primarily via passionate e-mails—until Alan paid a visit to Diane at her home, and Scott subsequently read about the visit in a titillating e-mail.*
>
> *Scott's voice on the telephone rattled with rage as he said that just imagining another man in his own bed had been the last straw. He'd confronted his wife, and she'd been defiant, accusing Scott of trying to control her. Scott and Diane have been married for only four years and have no children.*
>
> *My first question to each in therapy is, "Why are you here?"*
>
> *"I'm here to save my marriage," says Scott, sounding exasperated at the question.*
>
> *"I'm here because Scott asked me to come," says Diane.*

After thanking Diane for her honesty, I tell her that coming to therapy only in response to Scott's request is not a good enough reason. I go on to explain that when a husband and wife come for counseling, I assume I'm present to help the two of them heal their marriage. That makes the marriage my primary client. Therefore, I expect and require the active participation of both spouses during each step of the healing process. When I ask whether each understands and agrees to this role, Diane makes a detour and offers up one of her primary complaints in the marriage.

"We never talk. He just walks in the door and goes into his office."

"I don't ignore you all the time, just when you cheat on me."

"We can look at your communication problems next. But our first order of business is whether you're seriously interested in healing your marriage."

After Scott and Diane agree to this as the premise for the time we spend together, I turn to Diane and ask the next important question. "Diane, are you willing to break off your affair with this man, Alan?"

Although she says nothing, Diane's body language—arms crossed and held tightly against her chest, clenched jaw and gaze held steady on the blank wall—suggests this is not an easy decision for her.

Diane responds. "The whole thing happened accidentally. Anyway, I hardly see him. There's nothing to end."

"Do you see why it's impossible for you and Scott to work on your marriage if he can't trust the fact that it's over between you and Alan?"

"Yeah, I guess."

After Diane agrees to end the affair, Scott pointedly asks how he's supposed to know if Diane is telling the truth.

I suggest that Diane put her statement to Alan in the form of an e-mail or a phone call. I explain that she must tell Alan to stop all contact with her, and make it clear to Alan that she's decided to work on her marriage. Then she has to firmly let him know the affair is over. To reassure Scott, I tell Diane she can consider showing Scott this e-mail exchange between she and Alan or allow Scott to be in the room when she makes the phone call to Alan. At our next session, Diane announces she's ended her affair with Alan. Scott appears satisfied with Diane's actions, and, as a result, he's removed the tracking software he'd put on Diane's computer to spy on her.

At the beginning of their relationship, Scott says and Diane concurs, their sex life was great, and they enjoyed each other's company. Even food shopping was fun, together. When I ask Diane to describe the beginning of the marriage, she brightens, describing how Scott used to be into the "romance thing," surprising her with gifts, and complimenting her appearance, which pleased her. He doesn't do that anymore, she adds.

The process is tenuous. The path is filled with landmines.

"Diane, I want you to say aloud everything you love about Scott."

"Oh," she says, apparently thrown by my request. "Well, he's smart, and funny. At least he used to be."

"That's a start. Scott, now it's your turn."

"She's very feminine. I like that."

The exercise goes on from there, as each spouse excavates layers of anger and hurt in order to rediscover and reclaim the love that was once there. Diane and Scott had to "reset" their relationship by remembering what it was that brought them together in the first place.

Without recovering this emotional foundation of their marriage, the hard work of forgiveness and learning new communication skills would be too daunting. Diane and Scott's work in therapy had barely begun, but the immediate purpose—to stabilize the marriage—had been accomplished.

For a marriage to stabilize after an episode of infidelity two things must happen. First, the one having the affair must agree to stop it.

There is no room for gray here; if the affair continues the marriage will break down. Second, there must be a commitment from both partners to work on saving their marriage. After that, the process of communication can begin again from a more positive ground.

For a typical couple in this situation, Stephen Martin finds that six to ten sessions of marital therapy are usually sufficient to get them back on the right track. After this period, a typical couple has a much greater ability to deal with problems before they escalate into a marital crisis. As the old saying goes, "To give a man a fish is to feed him for a day. But if you teach him to fish, you feed him for life." A smart couple gets their fishing line in place early in a marriage.

The One Who Goes Outside the Marriage

The future of a marriage in the aftermath of an episode of infidelity can depend upon whether the one who cheated genuinely sees the pain her action caused the other spouse. Simply witnessing or acknowledging your partner's pain without being defensive about your actions is an important step. It's through vulnerability and remorse, sharing pain, and offering new affirmations of love that marriages are rejuvenated.

The One Who Stays Behind

Recovering from an episode of infidelity is never an easy process. And, fair or not, it's often much harder for the person who has been on the receiving end of the infidelity. The key factor in his response is whether he can openly display the pain he feels. For a man, this can be especially hard.

At the same time, it's important to recognize that infidelity never occurs in a void, and then be open to seeing your own part in creating the situation. You may need to acknowledge aloud to your partner that your own negative behaviors—whether you were overly critical, sexually withholding, or unwilling to deal with emotional conflict—contributed to his going outside the marriage to satisfy unmet needs. In this way, the crisis becomes an opportunity for renewal of the relationship.

Infidelity as a Symptom of Another Problem

Although some sexual straying outside a marriage, particularly when someone indulges in a one-night stand, can be viewed as a biological response to an opportunity presenting itself, an extramarital relationship of any duration is often a reflection of something askew in the emotional health of the primary relationship. Communication between the two partners has almost certainly broken down. Sexuality may also be unsatisfactory to one or both.

People often lack insight into their own behavior. If a man does understand *why* he cheated on his wife, he may not want to disclose this information to her; he may think that doing so will only cause more problems. However, if she already knows about the affair, and the underlying issues are not identified, the emotional health of the marriage will only deteriorate further and faster if he doesn't come clean with what he knows about his own feelings and motivations. Quite often, marriage counseling is the best way to identify the underlying problems and begin to attack them.

Should You Tell?

This brings up the often controversial question of whether telling a spouse that you had an extramarital affair (particularly a brief one) is always the best way to go. The underlying question is whether keeping this secret undermines the relationship any more or less than spilling the beans might. In Stephen Martin's view, although honesty is the best approach, if the man or woman who strayed stops all contact with the other person, and decides to remain in and work on his marriage, therapy can sometimes better address the underlying problems in a marriage without the added drama caused by the confession of an affair.

In fact, there are times when such confessions can be self-indulgent on the part of the unfaithful spouse, more designed to relieve guilt than improve the marriage. Marriage therapists and experts differ widely on this issue. Ultimately, whether or not to confess an affair, or the temptation to enter one, is an individual decision to be made in your own heart and mind.

Dealing with Emotional Infidelity

In the murkier area of what some call nonsexual infidelity, it is similarly difficult to definitively spell out right or wrong except on an individualized basis. When it comes to friendships with members of the opposite sex outside of marriage, there is only what feels right and what works for the two people who are married to each other. This is something the two of you can only arrive at through communication and negotiation.

Once again, therapists and marriage experts differ on this issue. Some hold that any and all flirting or socializing with a member of the opposite sex constitutes a threat to marriage and should be discouraged. Stephen Martin points out that how comfortable or distressed one partner becomes as a result of the other's social behaviors often depends on how secure she feels about herself and her marriage. On the other hand, he says, if the distressed partner feels her partner is giving or getting from a third party what she feels is missing from their own relationship, for example an emotional closeness that used to be present, that is solid ground from which to confront a partner and ask that his attentions be turned back homeward.

This set of issues underscores the need for partners to agree upon the amount of togetherness and separateness that works for both individuals in the marriage. It also relates to the absolute need for clear emotional boundaries to exist between two married people—in other words, what each of them needs emotionally from the other. This area is explored more thoroughly in Chapter 11.

Abandonment

When infidelity brings up violent feelings of jealousy in a spouse, there is often within this intense reaction a fear of abandonment similar to the reaction of a baby who instinctively fears being left by his mother. Before the marital problems exposed by infidelity can be dealt with, it's sometimes necessary for the spouse who's been left behind to deal with her own overpowering feelings, including abandonment. When someone looks closely at emotions, his own and those of others, he often finds that much human behavior stems unconsciously from the fear of abandonment, which is in turn rooted in early childhood experiences.

The truth is that all people have these dark feelings to manage. Like greed, lust, and the other negative feelings, jealousy can express itself in self-destructive ways. To cope with these feelings it is best to look them straight in the eye. Do not run from them. Understand them. Learn how to manage them, and accept that all humans have a fear of abandonment and loneliness to deal with, and often these feelings are hard to work through.

Rebuilding Trust

If both parties decide to try and save a marriage troubled by an episode of infidelity, the next phase is often the most difficult. To begin with, it requires an understanding of the motivations underlying the affair. Both partners must then take a look inside and determine their own parts in creating the faulty dynamic in the relationship. They must then take concrete steps to change those factors that led the unfaithful partner to cheat.

 **Alert**

Research shows that married people are physically healthier than their single counterparts. People who stay married live, on average, four years longer than the unmarried.

In addition to identifying the motivations underlying the affair, it may be essential to the one who stayed behind to have the one who strayed candidly discuss the details of what happened. Again, most cheating spouses attempt to hide the details of the affair, thinking that telling the truth will only lead to more problems. Actually, concealing the details of the affair can lead to lingering questions, which, if not addressed, may not go away on their own. If questions linger, it can be difficult for the hurt spouse not to continue dwelling on the affair. This is another individual decision. The request for more details about the affair should come from the spouse who is having trouble trusting the partner who had the affair.

Forgiving the Unforgivable

It would be hard to define a single more important key to finding happiness in marriage than forgiveness. Forgiveness is the art of letting your mind rest around issues that are troubling to you. When the mind is engaged with the tension about wrongs and hurts you have suffered in the past, your mind is in torment. Thus, the ability to rest your thoughts about past hurts gives you inner peace and mental rest.

However, this begs the question of how do you learn to forgive? How do you stop fearing the future? When you hurt another person, guilt is the dominant emotion. When you believe others have hurt or wounded you, anger is the usual response. Either way, your mind is unsettled and troubled. Forgiveness rests the mind and settles the past, allowing you to live in the present moment without the pain and the torment of those past hurts, and without fear of the future.

 Question

How can I survive my partner's infidelity?
Not by sitting on your anger or trying to forget what happened. A positive outcome after the pain of infidelity requires an unbreakable commitment between the two of you to work through the issues that created the crack in your relationship.

The Mechanics of Forgiveness

Many people successfully use rituals to learn how to forgive. Some seek the use of confession. Others talk in therapy. Some write letters to people who have hurt them in the past, expressing all their feelings, and then never send the letter. This way, they can unburden their feelings about the past without involving all the people who have made up that past. Another ritual might be to dig a hole in the earth and shout your hurts into that hole, at the same time releasing the pain of that hurt. Then you can cover the hole, and send the hurt away. Such rituals are physical tasks to help you grasp the emotional aspect within the act of forgiveness.

 **Alert**

Words matter. To better communicate your needs and feelings without making your partner feel defensive, start statements with "I" and choose feeling words. I feel. I need. I'm sorry. I appreciate.

Forgiveness is letting your mind release the emotional turmoil that you are holding onto, but the real key to understanding forgiveness is to recognize that you as a human have no ability to forgive anyone but yourself. Your forgiving another is not about them at all, it is entirely about you and your mental process. You let go of the tension you hold in your mind about that person. You let go the inner turmoil you feel, and thus you allow yourself to experience emotional rest and mental peace. You don't even need for them to ask forgiveness, or to apologize—although in the case of infidelity, sincere apologies do make a difference.

To forgive is to bless yourself. To forgive is to grant yourself freedom. To forgive is to give yourself the gift of happiness, because when you release the inner tension, you release your mind from the torment you have been carrying by not forgiving yourself or another. To forgive another does not require that they apologize or repent. To forgive is to release the inner tension you carry when you hold hatred within your heart for those who have wronged you. Forgiveness is moving on. In a marriage healing from infidelity, it is also the key to allowing the marriage to move on, too.

Why Couples Stay Together after an Affair (Most Do)

Most married couples stay together after an episode of infidelity because the partners believe that their love and the commitment made to the marriage are of greater importance than the affair. Of course, this assumes that the affair is over and that another affair does not take its place. The process of rebuilding trust is often lengthy. If the couple uses the crisis brought about by an extramarital affair as an opportunity to learn from their mistakes, to improve their communication, and to renew their sexuality, the marriage will be stronger than it was before the crisis occurred.

 Question

Why do people stay together after an affair?
Because forgiveness is a muscle that must be exercised, for the sake of the children and for all they've built together. Just as important, they stay together because once the difficult issue between them has finally been forced out into the open, they have a real chance to get the love they've wanted from each other all along.

Affairs happen in marriages of all lengths. Very often, the feelings brought up in both partners—the one who cheats and the one who feels betrayed—were lurking below the surface, subverting the relationship for some time prior to the affair. While it would be better to approach unresolved issues without the drama and pain inflicted on both partners by one's affair, some people simply can't or won't deal with difficult emotions until or unless they have to.

When faced with the hurt and pain he's caused his wife, a wandering husband may finally have to ask for what he's been missing sexually and emotionally from his wife. The same goes for a straying wife.

Chapter 11

The Self in Marriage

LOVE IS NOT really love if it's not freely given. If you are unhappy, your partner cannot make you happy by loving you more, or in a way more to your liking. Neither can you make him happy. To have a successful marriage, each partner must accept personal responsibility for her feelings, self-esteem, and state of being. Each partner must also accept the consequences of her behaviors. Making your happiness his responsibility inevitably leads to misery for both of you and puts your marriage into a state of perpetual conflict. This chapter contains some cautions and suggestions to help you avoid falling into this common relationship trap.

Have a Blissful Union . . . Without Losing Yourself

"The two shall become one." So says the Bible in Mark 10:6–9. The merging of two hearts and two souls remains the blissful ideal vision for most people entering "the state of holy matrimony." Bliss is a noble goal for any marriage. Instead of heaven on earth, though, half of those who marry find themselves in something closer to a living hell—within seven years. What happens to all those vows of "till death do us part?" There's no doubt that most couples begin married life optimistic that they'll be among those who'll make it. So what is it that goes so terribly wrong?

The problem with this ideal for marriage—one that melds romantic love with spiritual bliss—is that unless both partners enter a marriage as whole and independent people, the union is inevitably flawed and deeply troubled. In order to attain a blissful marriage, you must accept responsibility for your own happiness and then embrace the process of setting emotional boundaries between the two of you, leaving room for individual self-growth. Then yes, create space for the two of you to grow together as a married couple. Both steps are necessary. These are not easy goals, just essential ones.

 Question

What is a boundary?
A boundary is a statement of what you will and won't do for or with your partner. It's a decision about what you're willing to put up with, and what you won't tolerate in the marriage. Think of the process of boundary setting as working preventively to come up with a list of actions or omissions that fall into either the "yes" or "no" column; in other words, the point where you cross over the line to irreconcilable differences.

Most young people, and many older ones who should know better, hold their marriage partner responsible for their individual satisfaction. While marriage can be a factor in achieving happiness, alone it will never guarantee fulfillment. In marriage, like the rest of life, happiness is "an inside job." With all the emphasis on marital bliss, it's understandable if this concept is still a bit fuzzy for many people. You may not even be conscious of exactly when and how you go about projecting your unhappiness onto your partner.

Here are some common examples of relationship dynamics that reflect these unconscious projections:

- A man who tries to fill his emptiness by attempting to control his wife's appearance
- A woman who attempts to cover her inner void by demanding more and more of her husband's romantic attention and adoration
- A man who feels like a professional failure, and then seeks constant approval from his wife to make up for these painful feelings
- A woman who measures her husband's love by whether he agrees to accompany her to a party he doesn't wish to attend

All of these issues or situations can be addressed if the partners are honest about their feelings and willing to compromise. Another equally important factor for untangling destructive dynamics such as these is making sure each one knows when a particular compromise may not be possible—when differences become irreconcilable.

Reconcilable Differences

Most often, it's the unconscious, unspoken conditions people set for the marriage and each other that get relationships into trouble: The man who believes that being married means he'll never feel lonely, or the woman who depends on her husband's compliments in order to feel good about herself, or anyone who believes that being married means you'll always get sex when you want it. Sometimes the only way to discover which unconscious projections or unspoken agreements may be operating in your relationship is by paying attention to the issues you tend to fight about most often.

For example, when a woman habitually feels unappreciated, it may be a signal that she's projecting her unhappiness onto her husband, particularly when, if she doesn't get a compliment, she then finds her day "ruined." Of course any relationship takes two, and given the habitual quality of this husband-and-wife dynamic, one wonders if he is more of a nonverbal person, not given to saying what he thinks or feels, or, alternately, whether this husband may have unexpressed anger toward his wife that he's acting out by withholding the common courtesy of expressing appreciation.

As you can see, just because these two spouses have a running argument about expressing appreciation, their fights can only serve as red flags. If the partners want to get to the bottom of this conflict, they will have to take a closer look at the dynamics involved, perhaps with the help of a third party. As any marriage therapist will concur, problems in marriages are not always what they appear on the surface. This is why regular check-ins and emotional honesty are so important for couples if they are going to navigate the tricky waters of emotional boundaries in marriage. If they can't get to harmony on their own, then they should consider visiting a therapist for assistance.

 **Alert**

Why do most marriages self-destruct? Because one partner makes the other responsible for his happiness and personal fulfillment.

The Importance of Making Clear Agreements

Any relationship dynamic from the outside can be given a simplistic analysis. For example: the man who won't accompany his wife to the party is being selfish and withholding. But one could just as easily conclude that this man's wife is being self-centered since she knows he doesn't want to go to the party. Had she even considered going without him? What is or isn't true in this situation depends entirely on the agreements this couple has or hasn't made—assuming they've ever made agreements about socializing together and apart.

If this couple has discussed the topic of their social lives, each may agree that it is acceptable to socialize separately. Or, they agree that it's okay to go out separately other nights but they'll always socialize together on Saturday nights. Another problem ensues if the wife makes this single incident a test of her husband's love. . . . "If he really loved me, he'd put aside his other feelings and come to the party." This and many other common marital dilemmas can be averted or minimized if the two partners sit down and make boundaries and agreements a regular topic of discussion.

E ssential

Couples get in trouble when they assume questions about how to conduct their married life are simply understood, without discussion or agreements being made. Think about it: You would never assume a business partner should read your mind about how to operate the business. You would discuss the pros and cons and make a joint decision. Married life needs the same level of cooperative thought and behavior.

Problems from Blurred Boundaries

One reason couples have such a hard time establishing and observing boundaries in marriage is because of the broader culture of blame and victimization they live in that shapes their attitudes and expectations for marriage. The American legal system is set up around this premise. If someone is wronged, he hires a lawyer who will fight for his rights in court to prove one right and the other wrong. Or, at least to show one more right, and the other more wrong.

Once you accept this premise, it is easy to understand how, inside marriage, whenever one party feels unhappy, she might assume that her partner is in some way responsible. Then, believing that all the negative feelings she experiences are her partner's fault, the fighting begins. Eventually that fighting takes on a life of its own. Fueled by a cultural belief that one is right and the other is wrong, obviously, it is you who are right, and your partner who must be wrong. If you believe your feelings are your partner's responsibility, the marriage can never improve until your partner changes. At this point, the marriage goes down the slippery slope into despair.

Don't Be a Victim

Is there an alternative to this system? Of course there is. The solution is for each of you to take full responsibility for your own feelings, and not project your unhappiness upon a partner. Once you become aware that you are internally dissatisfied, it becomes your responsibility to make a change in order to fix that unhappiness. If you see yourself as a victim of your partner's behavior, this establishes a classic power struggle that eats away at the good inside your marriage and dooms the relationship—unless your partner passively accepts all the blame for all your problems. Once this occurs, however, you risk losing all respect for your partner and becoming bored and disinterested in the relationship. You will inevitably label your partner emotionally weak or passive-aggressive.

The victim-perpetrator model for human relationships guarantees the relationship will fail. This is not to say that you should keep silent about where you feel wronged or that you cannot request your partner consider a change if it is realistic. That is perfectly acceptable communication, as long as it is delivered responsibly and in an adult fashion. Many couples lash out at each other when angry, just like a child might throw objects at another child when he feels overwhelmed. The good news is that these skills can be learned. Once learned, the skills become "love acquired by habit," meaning practice.

Balancing Conditional and Unconditional Love

No matter how much you believe your love for your partner is unconditional, love is almost always conditional. Unconditional love is an ideal, rarely obtained by mortal beings.

Clearly love exists on a continuum between the unconditional and the conditional. Conditional love in the extreme is very unappealing: The person is not being loved for who he is; he's loved only if he fulfills the requirements set forth by his partner. In reality, total conditional love is not love at all; it's closer to slavery. Unconditional love is an ideal no one can achieve. However, there are aspects of unconditional love that are very appealing. Perhaps the best statement defining a realistic version of unconditional love is, "I love you for who you are, and for who you are not." It acknowledges that the one offering love has judgments and requirements that they're attempting to minimize, or go beyond. This is the beautiful quality of love that is acceptance. And perhaps that is the best we can ever achieve. Acceptance of who the other is recognizes that he has free will and his choices may not always be what his partner wishes—and yet, you love him.

 Fact

A healthy marriage is one where both of you are better people as a result of the marriage.

Love offered with too many conditions places expectations upon others that can never be totally fulfilled. When you have expectations, you are setting yourself up for disappointment. Thus, the best form of love minimizes judgments, conditions, and expectations. Complete unconditional love is unattainable, but, as an ideal, it is useful if it encourages couples to work toward mutual acceptance. Not that there won't be expectations; everyone is human. You will simply own your own expectations and attempt to move beyond them.

Behind the Need to Control Your Partner

Once you fall in love—unless you're the unusual human being who's done all the emotional work required to be fully conscious of her projections—the immature part of you begins thinking in terms of power and ownership. This is the part of you, as discussed previously in this chapter, who believes that, once you get married, you'll never be lonely again. With this premise operating in the back of your mind, you attempt to control your partner, storing up hurt and resentments when he doesn't fulfill your immature expectation. Your love begins to buckle under the weight of this onerous burden.

You become even more needy, asking for more of his attention, more proof of his love and adoration, until he feels so overwhelmed, he concludes you'll never be satisfied—and eventually quits trying to please you. Marital stalemate achieved. Although you might not recognize this common dynamic as an attempt to control your partner—in other words, a marital power grab—it is precisely that. Control is an expression of power, asserted without full agreement by both parties. Usually one person in a dependent relationship wishes for more control than the other and this is when the real problems emerge.

 Question

How does the issue of control show up negatively in a marriage?

The controlling spouse is usually the insecure one, and this partner can be either male or female. In attempting to deal with her insecurities, insidiously, she makes it seem as though the problem belongs to her partner. "You don't love me enough," or "You need to check in with me before you make any personal decisions" are often the controlling partner's attempts to limit the other's individual decision making and thus manipulate him into doing what she wants. This power play within marriage can tear apart trust, fun, and aliveness.

Control is very deceptive. It hides in many forms. For example, one partner can control another by positioning himself as emotionally weak or helpless within the relationship. Threatening to fall apart if the partner leaves him is an attempt to exercise control. It may be difficult to see this as controlling behavior, for the one doing the threatening may be convincing when he seems so helpless. Yet, in reality, he is expressing the desire to hold onto the relationship by making threats.

When Control Shows Up as Jealousy

Another way to control a partner is through jealousy, specifically by allowing it to run amok. Many people believe that jealousy is an expression of love. Not so. When there is no issue of infidelity, jealousy is often a way to control your partner. You may feel as though you cannot bear to have him move away or leave you, or watch him share some part of himself with someone else. Jealousy, in the extreme, is controlling behavior that will eventually destroy the fragility of love by giving in to one person's insecurity and by thwarting the other person's freedom.

Like control, jealousy can also be deceiving. It is easy to blame your partner for the jealous feelings you may experience. Rather than accept jealousy for what it most often is (insecurity), the jealous partner can attempt to prove you untrustworthy, and thus responsible for the jealousy. With jealousy disguised as a trust issue, the jealous partner does not have to own his feelings of insecurity. The message then is "Your behaviors are the cause of my jealousy" rather than "My insecurities are creating emotional distress within me, and I would like your assistance with this issue."

 **Alert**

When you don't like who you've become as a result of being married to your partner, the marriage is unhealthy.

This is not to suggest that you are not responsible for being very considerate of your partner's emotional needs. That is the very essence of love. Consideration, compassion, and concern are critically important elements in a marriage. That said, love can never be mandated. Love will not survive the controlling nature of jealousy and possessiveness. When love loses its freedom, love begins to disappear.

Here is another excerpt from the case of Scott and Diane, the couple first introduced in Chapter 10. This section focuses on the lack of emotional boundaries in the relationship, an issue that became clear in the aftermath of the crisis wrought by Scott's discovery of Diane's infidelity.

When we spoke by telephone, Scott informed me that Diane refused to come back to marriage therapy and, in fact, now blamed me, the therapist, for the problems in their marriage. This is not unusual. In fact, it's further evidence of Diane's refusal to take responsibility for her own emotions and actions. At this point, my role with Scott and Diane changed. I would now be helping Scott confront his own issues, in effect, the fallout of his (perhaps temporarily) broken marriage. Over the course of four sessions, Scott and I spoke very little about Diane. Our agenda had become Scott, as I sought to show him how his need to control Diane now fit the description of an addiction. The addiction had been exposed by the emotional struggle in his marriage, but it was important for Scott to see that the issue had been there for much of his life. The adoration he once received from Diane had served to hide Scott's emptiness. It was this hole in himself, not Diane's actions or her apparent lack of love for him, Scott now confronted.

In an important first step, Scott finds that he can change his response to Diane's actions—for example, by not following the inclination to spy on her. When Scott deals with the anxiety prompted by his suspicions by doing something he enjoys—shooting hoops with a friend from work—he finds that he immediately feels better. He manages to forget about Diane's betrayal for minutes or hours at a time. It's important to note that such small steps can make all the difference in personal growth. Nothing about Scott's transformation is going to be quick or easy. But, because he's now dealing with the only thing he has any real power over—his own thoughts and actions—it will be a productive journey. Meanwhile, if Scott is going to stay in his marriage, he will have to set boundaries in his relationship with Diane. If he can't tolerate what she now describes as a nonsexual "friendship" with Alan, he has two choices: he can try to change his response to this issue, or offer Diane an ultimatum. And then stick to it.

Scott and Diane's marital problems provide a vivid illustration of the reality that without self-love there can be no love between two people, and certainly no bliss in marriage.

 Question

What is the difference between loneliness and solitude in a marriage?
Loneliness is an emotionally painful experience that may be an important indication that you've become socially isolated or overly dependent on your partner for friendship and approval. Solitude is a choice to be alone for any purpose, such as self-examination, relaxation, recreation, or renewal.

Together and Apart

Like every married couple, you and your partner will have to wrestle with how much is enough togetherness—and what constitutes too much. There are as many answers to this question as there are marriages. Your agreement on this subject is also likely to change over the course of your marriage, as each of your individual needs and the needs of your family shift. Problems arise when you and your partner disagree about the right balance of togetherness and separateness in your marriage. Take heart—very few couples begin in the same camp on this issue. What successful couples know is that the balance of togetherness and separateness is an issue they must keep on the table for ongoing discussion and compromise through-out their marriage.

Feelings of loneliness can also indicate another, more personal, problem that results from not liking your own company. If this is true of you and you haven't yet come to terms with your dilemma by going to individual therapy or taking other constructive steps, there is a danger that you will project your unconscious feelings of poor self worth onto your partner; in other words, you may believe he doesn't love you when in fact the problem is that you don't love you. At the base of loneliness is poor self-esteem.

Essential

Good self-esteem in both partners is the essential foundation for a healthy marriage. By combining two insufficient halves you do not get a whole. Only two whole people can form a happy, emotionally healthy relationship.

The Joys of Solitude

Loneliness stems from facing uncomfortable feelings that you may not be able to avoid when no one else is around to distract you from them. Solitude, on the other hand, is being comfortable with oneself. It is a time to relish your own thoughts and your own experiences. Solitude can be a time for self-renewal, for generating new ideas, for meditating on personal goals, and for creating a course for the future. It is in solitude that personal creativity occurs. People who do not understand solitude tend to fear it. The belief is that in solitude you are alone and lonely. Partnering is a wonderful way to grow and develop the side of you that needs interaction with other humans, but solitude is just as valuable and just as rewarding. Solitude may need to be scheduled if you find yourself driven and too busy. Without time for self, the batteries run down and the light begins to fade. Just as we need solitude, people also need companionship.

Everything in life requires balance to be healthy. Balance provides us with the harmony we need to be emotionally healthy. However, it is also true that when many people are with others, they are not getting or giving enough of themselves to experience true intimacy. Solitude is essential for healthy human development, but so is real intimacy with real sharing. It is in the mix that people, and especially those attempting to make marriage work, find optimum opportunity.

With such busy lives it's equally important to schedule time for solitude and time to be together with your committed partner. Many couples do this best by sharing a common adult interest that they do regularly together, be it golf, the symphony, motorcycle riding, or birding. This is not the same as attending children's sporting activities or recitals together as that falls into the category of family time. The important thing about couple togetherness is to make sure this time is solely about sharing something you enjoy doing as a couple. Make it fun for both of you; then it will be easy to keep it up as a habit for life.

Chapter 12

Marriage and Children

THE BIGGEST MISTAKE you can make as parents is sacrificing your marital relationship to what you perceive as the greater needs of your children. In fact, if you let your marriage suffer, you are doing your children a far greater disservice. Your children rely on the strength of your marital relationship as much or more than each of you do. In this chapter you'll find some tools for keeping your marriage strong while you raise healthy, well-adjusted children.

Parenting as a Team

In parenting, as in other areas of life, it is normal to rely upon past experience to shape your future expectations. Most people enter marriage believing their parents' marriage and the child-rearing style by which they were raised is the right model to follow with their own kids. Many times this is true. The opposite situation is just as common, where you grew up with parents who had a bad marriage and an equally poor parenting style. Before you take on the job of parent, it's important to review your personal history and take stock of the emotional baggage you may be carrying (everyone has some) from your parents' successes and failures.

The second most important thing you can do, if you haven't done so already, is share what you come up with in a relaxed, intimate conversation with your partner. When both of you come to terms with your own personal stories, and then reveal them to each other, it will be easier to agree on where you wish to go together—as parents. The two of you should then make a commitment to read as many books on child development and discipline as you possibly can, take parenting classes (preferably together), and communicate clearly about all aspects of the game plan you will follow as parents.

Parenting is a task no one is ever prepared for or adequately trained in. Neither life nor parenting begins with a manual. When you accept that, you have the best chance at successfully learning how to be a good-enough parent. One pitfall many couples fall into is aiming for perfection as parents. Simply put, the goal of parental perfection is a fantasy. As such it can be self-indulgent, impossible, guilt inducing, and even destructive for both parents and children. So, when you begin to feel overwhelmed with the task of parenting, and unsure that you are doing it right, that's a good thing. Because uncertainty and inadequate training is where everyone begins this task.

Partners Before Parents

Your first test as new parents is adapting to the changes children bring to your marital relationship. In a word, this adjustment is monumental. Studies show that marital satisfaction drops significantly after the birth of the first child. This is mainly due to a lack of mental and emotional preparation, especially on the part of the husband who doesn't realize (until he's feeling neglected and miserable) that it is entirely normal during the first six to twelve months after a new baby arrives for the husband to move into the "number two slot" in his wife's attentions and affections. Fortunately, this situation usually balances out again as your child ages.

Good marriages that include children set expectations for family times, and for couple times, and then keep an appropriate balance between the two. There should be weekly dates for the couple to go out by themselves and be adult together, apart from the kids or kid-centered activities. Far too many couples give up one-on-one time with each other, and as a result neither the adults nor the children are served. As usual, it's a perpetual balancing act.

Weekly family time is also essential to create a health family. It may be best to schedule family time for the same night every week; that way everyone can look forward to it on a regular basis. Special meals can be planned where the children select and help prepare the food. Family games also promote family togetherness, as do repeating rituals on holidays and birthdays. All of these efforts to build a solid family with strong emotional ties will help when it comes time to discipline your children.

When Discipline Styles Differ

A general parenting principle on which most experts agree is that children need strong boundaries, otherwise known as rules for behavior. Where it gets trickier is choosing which boundaries to set and determining the consequences for crossing those boundaries. Another unanimously accepted parenting principle is that children need plenty of attention and support while growing up. However, when parents give too much attention to their children to the detriment of their own relationship, the children often become manipulative, and that can lead to disobedience. Such children often grow up hungry for love, and turn into young adults who look for that love in all the wrong places.

One of the hardest parts of being a parent is finding agreement with your partner about how to guide your children and when to discipline. A complicating factor in coming to terms with a conflict in parenting styles is that norms for child discipline tend to change across different times and cultures. Parents in the 1950s used a strict disciplining style only to create the rebellious baby boom generation of the sixties and seventies; many of whom then became the decidedly permissive parents of today's so-called boom-let generation.

Achieving agreement with your partner about the discipline styles you intend to use (or change to) with your children is a critical step to take that avoids or remedies such problems. Before you can agree on how you'll discipline, you must understand the types of discipline. There are three general styles of parenting:

- **Authoritarian parents**, reflecting a more "top down" model, expect to set forth rules that are not challenged, only obeyed. Children make few, if any, of their own choices. Punitive measures are taken if rules are disobeyed.
- **Permissive parents** tend to go to the opposite extreme and provide very little structure or boundary-setting for their children. Children are then given the power to make their own choices, often with the belief that such permission will encourage a child's creativity.
- **Authoritative parents** fall somewhere in the middle of these two poles; they set rules and enforce them but remain flexible and open to input from their children.

For many modern families, the authoritative model of parenting tends to create the most workable environment. Rather than a "you will do this" message from parent to child, in this model, a child is given autonomy and encouragement to learn self-discipline. At the same time, parents in the authoritative model have the ability to set limits and ground rules for the ways children will behave in the household.

The purpose of good parenting is to take a child from total dependency to independence. This process usually takes eighteen years. As a child matures, the parent needs to gradually transfer autonomy to the child, a process that many parents don't fully understand or find difficult. The hard part comes when child becomes an adolescent and begins to make mistakes. That's when it's critically important for him to learn the consequences of his actions and to feel any self-imposed pain, rather than remove the consequences of his mistakes. It's also critically important to be united with your spouse in this process, to speak with one voice.

Creating a Family Culture of Respect

The golden rule, "Do unto others as you would have others do unto you," if practiced, would end all misery and suffering at the hands of other humans. If children are going to have a chance at growing up to be more peaceful adults, the first place this golden rule must be established and taught is by parents in the home. Successful discipline of children requires a strong commitment to a family culture of absolute, inviolable respect for each member's safety and well-being.

This commitment to assuring that everyone in your family gets the same level of physical and emotional safety translates into a zero tolerance for verbal or physical assaults made to or from anyone in the family.

The unbreakable commitment to respect and safety must first be lived by parents within the marital relationship if it is going to be understood and imitated by their children. Here are some of the nuts and bolts of basic parenting that underline the commitment of respect:

- Don't give up your authority
- Don't bargain with your child
- Don't discipline until you are calm and without anger
- Don't show your anxiety or fears when disciplining
- Do model vulnerability and an ability to recover from your mistakes
- Do set clear limits
- Do make simple, clear statements
- Don't expect a "thank you" (at least not immediately)
- Do emphasize the positive

It can be a difficult balancing act for a parent to play the disciplinarian and still strike a positive tone with children, but always remember that by setting boundaries and keeping to them, you are giving your child an essential life lesson. Parental discipline leads the child to self-discipline; eventually he will be empowered by his own self-control.

The Challenges of Adolescence

A special word is needed about teenagers. Adolescence is a very difficult transition for both teenagers and their parents. These brand new adults have the minds of children but the bodies of adults. They have to manage insecurity, rebellious feelings, a need to feel accepted by their peers, and the painful bodily changes that are happening to them. To deal with these changes, teenagers develop a superficial arrogance with which they attempt to mask their confusion. Their lack of humility can be frustrating to parents, and can result in outbursts of rage that exasperate the entire family.

 Question

What are natural consequences and how are they used to discipline a child?

Natural consequences refer to what happens naturally after the child takes an action. If she's late for school, her teacher marks her tardy and after three times, she gets detention. Within the limits of reason and safety, natural consequences take the parent out of the equation and bring the child face to face with her outcomes of own actions.

How can you survive a child's adolescence and help him make the necessary transition from child to adult? There are three keys that should be considered. First, remember what is developmentally occurring to an adolescent during this time. He is facing a strange and frightening new stage of life while ending another much easier one. Childhood has passed, and adulthood is approaching. He is integrating concepts of self-determination, identity, responsibility, and all the mixed signals he's receiving are difficult to digest. One day he acts like a child, the next day he's an adult. Mood swings tend to be exaggerated. Arrogance is a defense against the significant amount of fear that lies just beneath the surface.

Parents need to carefully shift responsibility for control of a teenager's life. You must loosen up on the controls so he can have "dry runs" at the difficult lessons of self-determination. The objective is to help him reach total responsibility for his life. This needs to be accomplished by gradually giving him more responsibility, and, as he demonstrates responsibility, more personal choice and freedom.

The second key in coping with your teen is to pick your battles wisely. The wise parent knows when to let things be, and when to draw the line. Don't get caught up in her emotional excesses. She is looking to hook you into her personal drama, but it is important that you step aside (lovingly) and don't do it. The typical adolescent is frequently experiencing emotional extremes, and if the parents join her in these extremes, the entire family will become unstable and emotionally disturbed.

The third principle is to always reassure your teenager that you love her, regardless of what she does and says. Of course, that doesn't mean you won't discipline her when you have to. When as a typical teen she questions so much in her life, she becomes confused about thoughts and feelings—and as such is vulnerable to making poor judgments about her choices. A parent's calm, loving support and boundary-setting around important issues is the best guarantee that your teenager will succeed.

When Families Need Professional Help

Family therapists can help a family system function better when it's under stress. This stress can be the result of marital tensions or the problems of one or more of the children. Typically in family therapy, the entire family shows up in the therapist's office, and the interactions of the family are observed and guided by the therapist who acts as an outsider to moderate the family process. A skilled therapist must first assess how a given family functions. He must assess who is playing what roles inside the family unit. This assessment is perhaps the most important task for the therapist. Families typically have a leader (usually Mom or Dad, but it can sometimes be a powerful child) who will try to organize and lead the process.

Eventually the therapist must help the family redistribute power away from the individual who is leading the family, and allow each family member to feel safe enough to discuss her issues within the family before the entire group. His primary means to do this is by providing a safe environment in family therapy sessions where all family members can express their feelings and needs. Then it's the job of the therapist to help family members acquire new communications skills so that they can employ them at home.

 **Alert**

> The power arrangements of families are sometimes hidden from view. These roles have often been unconsciously assumed over time, as the family power dynamics have taken form. Sometimes a problem child is running the family. In other families, a rage-filled parent keeps everyone else under control.

Nuts and Bolts of Family Therapy

The process of healing takes time for a family that has been operating under stress. Family therapy is a process that requires each member's participation. Over several sessions, family members can learn how they function both positively and negatively with all the other members. When you first engage in family therapy, the therapist will function as an observer, a silent detached guide who is responsible for assisting the family to heal the broken parts of their relationships. After observing family dynamics in the context of therapy, the therapist will then play a more active role, interacting with the family and its members to encourage open communication and help each member function optimally.

The average number of sessions for family therapy is between six and ten, so you are not necessarily looking at a forever situation. Once the family is stabilized, the therapist can be used on an as-needed basis. A trusted therapist whom your family can see when in crisis is an important ally for a family.

E ssential

If you feel the therapist is not understanding you, or providing assistance, trust your instincts and move on. It may be that a therapist's style of rendering treatment is not a good match for your family. If you're not feeling comfortable after several sessions with a therapist, honestly tell him your concerns and tell him you will be looking for a new therapist. You will know within the first session of family therapy whether the therapist is the right fit for your family.

Why Go to Family Therapy?

Usually a family starts family therapy when parents need help managing the children or when one member of the family is in crisis. If only one family member is identified as the patient, other family members are hiding their feelings behind an assumed status as one of the "good" children in relationship to the "patient" or problem child. This unhealthy dynamic will first have to be exposed and unraveled. That's because in family therapy, the entire family is the patient.

For example, in one home where the mother and father argued frequently and loudly in front of their three children, their oldest son, sixteen-year-old Brandon, became the family's ostensible problem child. In a clear bid to get his parents' attention, Brandon broke into a school building and defaced classroom walls with spray paint, getting caught by a school janitor and turned in to the police. When the call from the police came, a new round of fighting between Brandon's parents ensued, each blaming the other for "Brandon's problem." This explosion of tension left Brandon's younger brother and sister feeling even more scared and alone. When Brandon's father went to collect his son from the police station, Brandon refused to see his father, saying he'd only go home with his mother. What was evident here in addition to Brandon acting out the family problem was his apparent need to choose between his parents in their ongoing hostilities. Obviously, the problem in this family did not belong solely to Brandon. This was a case where a juvenile court judge's order to send the entire family into therapy as part of its adjudication of Brandon's misdemeanor crime was a blessing in disguise for all.

 Fact

> The problem child, also called the black sheep, controls the family by acting as the center of attention for the entire family. Other family members may feel unimportant or unseen in this family dynamic because so much time and energy is taken up by the problem child. An effective family therapy process will stabilize this imbalance and teach everyone how to get their needs met.

In the case of Brandon's parents, the husband and wife required separate marriage therapy to address their inability to communicate and resolve marital conflicts. At the same time, the entire family received therapy so that the children's needs for safety and emotional support could be seen and heard by the parents. Ultimately, stability returned to this household.

Special Needs Children and Marriage

The definition of "special needs" used here is broader than how this label is typically applied. This section addresses common parenting and marital issues that arise from the challenge of two parents coping with a child or adolescent afflicted with a behavioral or mental health disorder, addiction, disabling physical illness, or disability. The truth is that whether your child is deaf, using drugs, anorexic, or emotionally troubled, the stresses and coping strategies for parents are more similar than different. Marriage is hard enough without adding the disruptions and stress caused by the demands of a child with a serious problem. When this kind of ongoing stress is present in a relationship, balancing the emotional ups and downs is challenging work.

Unfortunately, according to available statistics, the chronic stress it produces is more likely to cause a couple to pull apart than pull together. The divorce rate for marriages with a disabled child is estimated at between 50 and 70 percent. The only heavier stress on a marriage is the death of a child, which destroys 90 percent of marriages. After hearing all the bad news, couples should be forewarned that they must commit to do the hard work of finding a better solution to handle the inevitable stresses that will inevitably come up if your child's special needs are anything other than short-lived.

While the solution for marriages facing such a challenge appears obvious (that is, to cooperate and support each other while dealing with the painful or trying circumstances), reality reveals that this is far easier said than done. To face these challenges as a team is the ideal, but this is on-the-job training with very little available support for couples under such duress.

The Blame Game

It is pointless to assign blame, but it is also human. For many people encountering a stressful life situation—especially as the parent of a troubled child—it feels counterintuitive to simply accept what is and work from that base line. Individuals within a couple who are frustrated by a large amount of stress tend to wander unconsciously into assigning blame and then the problem begins to tear their marriage apart rather than bond them together.

This same blame dynamic can affect parents confronting any sort of crisis, but the most documented research has been done around parents dealing with the death of a child. The individuals within the couple are so overwhelmed that they often turn on each other rather than come together for the mutual support that will make the experience more bearable. For many couples, accepting the reality that a child has a potentially debilitating health or mental health condition can feel like a loss nearly akin to death. In this case, the loss parents might experience may be more the dream of the young adult they wished a child to become. It is painful for any parent to be forced to stand by, feeling powerless to lift any large burden from a child.

If you are going to survive this experience and grow as a marriage and a family, the way of cooperation and teamwork is the royal road. Starting with a strong marriage makes you better prepared for the stresses that arise when your precious child is afflicted with a serious problem, but through hard work and commitment even a less solid marriage can rise to the occasion.

How to Avoid the Blame Game

First, you must accept that blaming—even if you think your partner *is* the one at fault because of something he did or neglected to do—will always be counterproductive. So are beliefs and statements such as, "Your family is full of alcoholics, that's why . . ." or "If you had played ball with him more often he wouldn't have. . . ." Rather than help you cope with the reality of your experience, blaming your partner will only make things much worse.

It is not easy to avoid such mind traps. Men and women in strong marriages know these games are disastrous and learn to avoid them whenever their minds begin to go down that road. In these cases, rather than succumb to blaming, the stronger partner should (figuratively) hold the space open for peace to return rather than match his partner in assigning blame. The highest priority must be put on avoiding the infighting that can occur where one of you begins to blame the other for the problems present in your family. If blame arises, you need to find ways to release the stress and get back to cooperating and coparenting.

Guilt as a Marriage Destroyer

Another emotion that is very difficult for parents of a child with a serious problem, be it physical or emotional, is guilt. When guilt arises in one partner, it is very common for him to become angry with his spouse in order to relieve his own feelings of guilt—an emotional reaction that is most often not recognized for what it is: a projection of guilt. Many times guilt will show up this way because the pain of facing one's own guilt is too heavy. To distinguish between feelings of guilt and anger is difficult when you are on either side of a heated discussion.

The first step for couples dealing with these challenges is to simply accept the many conflicting feelings that arise from the stress level they are experiencing as parents of a troubled child, and allow each other the space to have these conflicting feelings. If your partner becomes angry with you, you should take an emotional step backward and try not to become defensive. This is the way to get closer to cooperation, without isolating yourself and thus creating more anger in the relationship.

Every married couple, including those without a special needs child in the family, needs time away from the role of mother and father in order to nurture their own relationship. When dealing with the extra demands that a problem in a child can place on parents and on the entire family, this tending of the marriage relationship is even more important. There are several proven therapy options that can help keep spouses from falling into the common traps of blaming each other for a child's problem or enabling the child's negative behaviors; both are detrimental and capable of wearing down a marriage and putting the family at risk of breaking apart. The most useful therapeutic options in this situation are marriage therapy and group therapy for couples.

Chapter 13

Marriage and Stepfamilies

IF YOU'VE REMARRIED and have kids, you're a stepfamily, also called a blended family. One in every three Americans is part of a stepfamily, either as stepparent, stepchild, or stepsibling, and the numbers have nowhere to go but up. That's because 89 percent of men and 79 percent of women remarry within five years of divorcing. Maintaining a strong marital bond in a blended family is a tough challenge, one that undoubtedly contributes to the 60 percent divorce rate for second marriages. This chapter highlights the pitfalls of making marriage work in a stepfamily and offers some tips for coping.

The Challenges of Blended Families

The many challenges of membership in a stepfamily can be summed up in one word: expectations. Far too many people enter a second marriage with disappointments from a former, failed marriage front and center in their minds and a host of unrealistic expectations going forward. You want to "do it right" this time. If you're still nursing wounds from your marital break-up, you expect his love and your new blended family to take away all that pain, putting happiness in its place. Starting a marriage with these shaky assumptions is like a taking a cross-country trip with the wrong map, doomed from the start.

The challenges of marriage in blended families fall into two main categories, financial and emotional.

Financial

If you (or your partner) share child custody with an ex-spouse, there are greater costs incurred for the support of two (perhaps three) households—customarily each child has a bedroom and a wardrobe in each home—along with the expense of transporting kids back and forth. Then there's child support, day care, and, eventually, hefty college tuitions—along with all the other costs of family life. For many exes, it's very hard to keep the management of these child-related expenses clean of the inky residue of your divorce.

Emotional

The bond between a parent and her biological child is different than between a stepparent and her stepchild, and this difference need to be recognized as such without the guilt that often accompanies unreal expectations that these relationships should somehow be equivalent or equal. You can strive to have the best possible relationship with your stepchildren, and hope that your combined brood will get along, but you must be realistic. None of this closeness and cooperation is a given. You have to work at it, and then sometimes, despite your best efforts, these relationships remain difficult.

 Question

How long does it take for a family to blend?
According to the Stepfamily Association of America, it takes on average from four to seven years for its adult and child members to feel safe and comfortable within a new blended family.

In the face of these challenges, the best and only solution is to keep your marital relationship strong. All of the difficulties present in any marriage, and the tough job facing any parent, are harder, and more critical to resolve in a blended family. Chief among these challenges are communication, keeping a united front on child discipline, and boundary-setting.

Letting Go of the Past

If one or both of you were previously married, you're especially likely to enter this marriage with a very strong desire to make things work out—so as not to face a second divorce. However, if you've never been part of a blended family before, much of what you're about to do is new, and requires a fresh approach. It also requires higher-level relationship skills than have been necessary in the past. For all these reasons, it's important to let go of any anger or regrets you may be carrying from a previous marriage, or prior relationship.

For example, with children from previous marriages present in your reconstituted household it will likely be a long time before you and your spouse will be able to savor much time alone in your marriage, and no amount of wishing can change that. In other words, you can't get the past back, not yours or his. Still, there are spouses who hold onto jealousy, insecurity, or anger about a current partner's past marriage, ex-spouse, or children with that ex—well into a new marriage.

In *Stepcoupling,* therapist Susan Wisdom, LPC, writes about the need for adults and children in blended families to identify unresolved issues or wounds originating in the past. These are the issues that tend to come up frequently and elicit highly reactive emotions in one person. The adolescent who feels habitually left out, overlooked, or less than other family members; the prepubescent girl who feels jealous of her father's relationship with his new wife; the wife who resents the time her husband spends with his daughter; or the eight-year-old who fights incessantly with a stepsibling are possible examples.

In her book, Wisdom points to the person who's experiencing the issue as the one with the responsibility for identifying and dealing with it, although parents would need to assist children and, if necessary, the entire family might go to counseling together. In therapy, it might come out that these feelings originated much earlier but have erupted with the extra stress placed on a family member by the remarriage of a parent, the entrance of stepsiblings into a household, or the acquisition of stepchildren by an adult.

Divorce a Spouse, Not Children

There's a general rule of thumb that an adult requires a minimum of three years following a divorce in order to emotionally recover; that is, before he's ready to detach from the last relationship and fully engage with a new partner. However, if you and your ex have children together, you will never be completely disconnected from each other. Each child-centered interaction following your marital breakup is an occasion to stir up whatever's unresolved between you—or lay it to rest. That just takes into account potential issues between the exes.

 Fact

Words matter. Don't ask your stepchild to call you "Mom" or "Dad." He's likely to feel that calling you that would be an act of disloyalty to his biological parent. If he chooses to do this on his own, by all means, respond positively. If not, calling you by your first name is a common solution.

A substantial amount of clinical experience and research shows that a child takes much longer to emotionally recover from divorce (when compared to his parents)—and some never do. This reality makes the aftermath of divorce and the creation of a new blended family a delicate, often painful, and lengthy transition for all concerned. In their landmark twenty-five-year study, *The Unexpected Legacy of Divorce*, Judith Wallerstein, Julia Lewis, and Sandra Blakeslee expose two long-held assumptions about the children of divorce as dangerously false. The first assumption is that divorce is at most a temporary crisis for children when parents go about a family breakup without rancor. The second is that with joint custody, adequate visiting, and child support, children of divorce will fully recover and be far better off than if they'd remained in an intact family with unhappy parents still married to each other. Contrary to these widely held beliefs, the study authors found that a significant percentage of those adult children of divorce surveyed experienced more learning, emotional, substance abuse, and relationship problems—when compared with their peers from intact homes.

These data suggest that if you're a parent in a blended family you may be dealing with long-term emotional difficulties in your stepchild or biological child as a result of her experience of divorce. The positive side to knowing this is that you can avoid unrealistic expectations that she will necessarily snap out of her sadness after a brief period of adjustment. Your child or stepchild may adjust without great trouble, but she may also be troubled and act out her emotional turmoil in the context of your new blended family and beyond.

 **Alert**

Every child of divorce wants her parents to get back together—no matter how much she likes her new stepparent. Many hold on to this wish well into adulthood. As a stepparent this is a reality to accept—not something to change or resist—especially if you wish to form a positive relationship with your stepchild.

Many children of divorce hold onto resentment toward the stepparent for many years. A prudent course for a blended family is to arrange individual psychotherapy for a child during and after her parents' divorce. The key to making a blended family work is to normalize the child's feelings of loss and anger and provide sufficient time and space for her grieving process.

To help adults and children make the difficult transition into a new blended family, the best course is to cultivate a civil relationship with your partner's ex-spouse (your predecessor), so there can be a minimum of tension between you. This will make many things easier, especially for the children. First, it will allow the ex to make tension-free parent-child visits at your home. Civility also makes it possible for all to assemble peaceably at children's birthdays, graduations, and other joint child-family holiday observances.

 Question

What should you do if an ex-spouse is openly hostile to you or your new partner?
Regardless of the ex's behavior, never rail or criticize the ex in front of your child or stepchildren. Try to shield children from any ongoing conflict between the adults. If arguing persists, limit contact and set clear boundaries with your ex. Suggest counseling for the entire blended family, the ex included.

Stepparenting as Art, Not Science

Begin by realizing that this is a difficult job for which you (like most stepparents) are not trained or well prepared. There are few rules and fewer absolutes in stepparenting. Know you are not likely to receive gratitude or warm fuzzy feelings in return for your efforts. Be prepared not to overreact when you are told, "You're not my mother/father. You can't tell me what to do." Do not let such comments deter you from the responsibility to be a parent to any and all children in your household. There can't be factions within a family. You sink or swim together.

Martha married John when she was twenty-six and John was twenty-eight and the single father of five year-old Phillip. Martha's mother warned her about the burden she was taking on as an unprepared instant mother to this rambunctious boy whose biological mother came and went unpredictably, often leaving an angry, newly abandoned child in her wake. But Martha, in the throes of new love and newly pregnant, forged ahead, thinking the baby would help bind her often-frazzled blended family together. The reality proved otherwise, with her stepson's refusal to listen to Martha and his frequent tantrums only worsening when combined with the jealousy he felt after the arrival of his new half brother Corey. At her worst, Martha found herself dead tired, holding a wailing Corey as she screamed in anger at Phillip, often banishing him to his room. On more than one occasion, Phillip opened his door long enough to scream back at her, "I hate you! I want my mommy," words that convinced Martha her situation was hopeless and that she was the worst stepmother in the world. By the time John would get home from work at night, Martha typically greeted him with ultimatums (that he "do something" about Phillip) and tears.

Looking back, those months were definitely the worst for the entire family, with increments of improvement coming as Martha got more sleep and learned to set clearer boundaries with her stepson. Little Corey's presence did in fact eventually help smooth out the household's rougher edges as the baby began to worship his big brother Phillip whose attention always brought Corey big smiles and easy laughter. However, Martha's realization about her lack of preparation and perspective as a stepmother came a couple of years later. It happened when she had to give then three-year-old Corey a time-out in his room for an incident of bad behavior. When an angry Corey slammed the door and screamed, "I hate you," at his mother, Martha heard herself saying calmly, "I know you feel that way now honey, but you won't after you calm down." Martha stopped in her tracks, realizing that way back when

Phillip screamed the same words at her she had immediately assumed she was a bad stepmother; when the truth is that children in the throes of tantrums say things that one should never take personally. Setting limits for a child is part of every mother or stepmother's responsibilities to her child.

Here are some guidelines for helping children and stepchildren adjust and thrive in a blended family:

- Put your marital relationship first; without it, the other relationships will fall apart
- Stand by your partner and present a united front when disciplining each child in the household
- Make time for activities involving the whole family
- Keep separate solo outings for biological parents and children to reassure the child he still has a special bond with his parent
- Gently guide your biological child toward a relationship with his stepparent
- Don't take it personally if your stepchild refuses your conversations or invitations or expresses a wish for his biological parents to reunite
- Encourage your stepchild's positive behavior rather than dwell on his negative behavior
- Don't yell, shame, or nag a stepchild; defuse a negative interaction by looking at your own behavior; and then do what you can to defuse the situation
- Let your child or stepchild take the lead in how much togetherness or intimacy he's ready for with his stepparent

The difficulties of adjusting, and the time needed by everyone to do so in a blended family, should not be underestimated. Given the varying degrees of emotional maturity present in young children, school-age children, teens, and young adults, expectations should be adjusted to meet specific developmental levels.

Of course, given the difficulties inherent in parenting adolescents, any stepparent should realistically expect the job to be harder with teenage stepchildren. If you're stuck in conflict with or about an adolescent's behavior, and particularly if your marital relationship is suffering, make family therapy an option.

 **Alert**

Don't get stepped on. In an effort to be liked by your stepchild you risk becoming a doormat. Children respect and ultimately trust the stepparent who sets clear boundaries and responds fairly and consistently to the children's behavior. Good parenting is also good stepparenting.

Money and Blended Families

The financial strain of sustaining multiple households in a stepfamily can be large. The payment of child and spousal support to an ex takes a huge chunk out of many blended family's household budgets, creating stresses, which can then become hostilities between exes and current partners. If these conflicts come up in your blended family, first know they are common. But that doesn't mean you can't work to defuse them. The best way to do that is by communicating honestly and often with your partner about the facts and your feelings about situations that arise. However, dumping or habitually complaining about an ex—yours or his—gets you nowhere, and can create a negative atmosphere in your home akin to an armed camp.

First and foremost, keep your children and stepchildren out of these tensions. Never use a child as a messenger or to deliver an ultimatum to an ex. Always maintain the integrity of a child's relationship with his biological parent, and keep the child neutral in all post-divorce financial matters.

A common question for parents in a blended family is who, meaning which parent, pays for what? Whether or not you put your income into "one pot," this can be a tricky issue to sort out. Do you, and the child's other biological parent, finance your own child's education, clothes, camp, and other costs while your partner takes care of his own (biological) child's needs? What about inheritances and insurance proceeds? While these issues are too complex to cover here, suffice to say that one solution may work for you and your partner at the beginning of your marital relationship, but it may evolve and change over time. Be sure to make revocable decisions wherever possible.

Essential

If economically possible, move your blended family into a new house, rather than moving new stepsiblings and a stepparent into an existing household that previously belonged to one partner. This way everyone starts fresh, with new rooms and attitudes to match.

In the more immediate sphere of household money management, it's important to allocate chores and allowances (if any) in a way that's fair and clear to all of your children. Even if a child lives with you part time, having chores will integrate her more organically into the household, and make her feel less like a visitor.

Parenting Stepsisters and Stepbrothers

Any combination of his, hers, and our children adds up to a challenging parenting task. Among the many possible issues are differences in styles of discipline, ways of expressing affection, housekeeping standards, levels of family togetherness, assignment of chores, money management, the roles of the other biological parent and grandparents, and the relative closeness of relationships between siblings as well as stepsiblings. A good source of help is your local chapter of the Stepfamily Association of America (*www.stepfam.org*), which offers helpful information on its website and has local chapters and networks of support for stepfamilies in each state.

New relationships between stepsiblings are often conflicted, with issues such as sharing a room, meals, and chores among the most difficult. You can encourage better relationships, but these tensions are harder for stepparents to affect. Still, positive family activities and meals together along with a family culture of safety and mutual respect go a long way toward stabilizing the home atmosphere. Again, have realistic expectations and give these relationships sufficient time to evolve. Some blended families employ regular family meetings to deal with conflicts, planning chores, and family activities.

At all times, support your partner in his dealings with his and/or your children, so that the two of you present clear boundaries for everyone's behavior. If you have disagreements about discipline, air them privately and present your decisions together. Some families elect to have each biological parent administer the discipline with his or her child, but this is a matter of choice. The important factor is unity as parents, and by extension, as a family.

Chapter 14

Marriage and In-Laws

FOR BETTER AND sometimes worse, you don't get your partner without getting his family, too. Good in-laws can make married life better. There's potentially more love and support for everyone. Of course, if his family is severely dysfunctional or his parents are openly hostile to you, getting his family is a bad bargain—and one that can weaken your marriage—unless handled constructively. Navigating relations with in-laws is one of the trickiest areas of married life, requiring forethought, courage, honesty, verbal agility, and clear boundaries. It also yields great potential rewards.

After the Wedding

Your relationship with his parents begins even before you meet them, starting as soon as he informs them of your special place in his heart. They will then have whatever reaction this news brings, based solely on the relationship between parents and their adult child. This means you will likely begin your relationship with your in-laws already in a box of their making. All of this should be taken into account when you consider how little the start of your relationship with your partner's mother and father has to do with you.

Of course, that doesn't mean you're helpless or can't determine how his parents will affect you and your household. It just points out that everyone brings into adulthood a complicated family history, with pre-existing tensions, unaddressed wounds, alliances, black sheep, and secrets. It wouldn't be a family if most or all of these elements weren't present. Because it's his family and not yours, you are in the unique position of having an outsider's (sometimes clearer) perspective on his family, just as he brings a fresh perspective to your family of origin.

Being in this outsider role is where all the potential for good and bad emanates from when it comes to in-laws. For example, you may be welcomed as a leavening influence if you bring a female perspective to a mostly male family, or vice versa. Your personality, whether reserved or outgoing, may also be just the right element to balance the pre-existing family mix. On the other hand, you may, through no fault of your own, represent a threat to the family's current way of doing things. Perhaps you're a straight shooter, and the unspoken rule in your in-laws' home is to mince words and ignore tensions. Conversely, they may relish a good debate, or tolerate emotional outbursts, while that behavior horrifies your more introspective temperament.

In whatever way the elements of personality and family style may eventually mix over time, how you fit in (or not) will be clear to you by the end of your first visit, whether it occurs before or after the wedding. Which is why, right from the start of your marriage, you need to establish realistic expectations of and clear boundaries with your in-laws. You must base these expectations and boundaries on your judgment of what sort of people your in-laws are, and how they behave toward you.

Examine Your Expectations

Be aware of your own family baggage when you begin this process. If you came from an emotionally difficult or neglectful upbringing, you may have a burning desire for a warm, loving family to fill this void. If your in-laws don't fulfill this dream you may take it personally and feel bad about yourself. Better to approach this new relationship with your partner's parents as you would any other new personal connection; be cautious at first, at least until you have cause to trust and confide in them. Conversely, don't assume just because you come from a different culture, class, or race that your in-laws will not be open to you. Expectations can get you in trouble if they cause you to miss the person standing right in front of you.

Your Partner's Relationship with His Parents Affects Your Marriage

It's understandable if you become distressed when and if you see the strong, self-possessed adult man you married suddenly transformed into a passive-aggressive little boy in the presence of his parents. If you feel as though your partner is falling back into the role of son at your expense, you need to first put the situation in context. He may not be conscious of his response to his parents. If he is aware of it, he may not like his behavior any more than you but may be unable to control it. Everyone carries unresolved issues from childhood. This only becomes a problem in your marriage if it prevents him from taking a necessary stand in support of you in relationship to his parents.

Another common parent-child dynamic that becomes unavoidably clear when meeting in-laws is the daddy's girl syndrome, which you may or may not have previously known to be part of your wife's character. Again, whether this becomes a quaint discovery about her or a threat to your relationship depends on how your wife and her father respond when you, as her new husband, are added to the family. If dear old Dad considers you an interloper or threat to his relationship with his daughter, there's bound to be friction. Again, the impact of this pre-existing dynamic on your marriage can be large or small depending on whether your wife treats the situation as an opportunity for emotional growth from Daddy's girl to woman.

The Unavoidable, Tough Challenges

Sometimes life hands one of your parents (and by extension you and your spouse) a curve ball. You will be severely tested if an illness, accident, or alcohol or substance abuse provokes a crisis with an in-law or adult sibling. If one parent passes away suddenly, the widow or widower left behind may become more needy or demanding of your partner's time or emotional resources. How much of your partner's time and how long this goes on are important factors in determining how you might feel about it.

 **Alert**

> The decision to have an elderly parent move into your household is a very, very complex one. It may be your first choice, and you may receive solid support for it from your partner. Be sure you discuss it thoroughly. Is one of you home during the day to provide care? What about costs?

Before an elderly parent joins your household, you may wish to explore other options that might be available, such as the possibility of private, insurance, or government assistance for a live-in helper. There may be a nearby assisted-living situation that would allow proximity and yet maintain independence for the elderly parent. Giving up independence is not easy for most adult children or the elderly parent.

All of these and other complex interpersonal dynamics come into play when dealing with in-laws and extended families. Confronting and dealing with them can represent avenues for personal growth as much as they also may present temporary challenges. In order for them to be positive growth experiences, these situations require a high level of communication and teamwork in your marriage.

The Most Challenging In-Law Problems

Your mother-in-law says you're spoiling the kids. Your father-in-law tells you how to manage your money, or criticizes your "lack of ambition" as a provider. Maybe your in-laws were hostile from the word go and make their disappointment with their son's choice of a wife clear at every opportunity. One mother-in-law does this by keeping a framed photo of her son's former girlfriend prominently displayed in her home—without one of you. Another father-in-law sends checks to his daughter but demands she keep these gifts secret from you—for fear you'll mismanage the money. All of these problems are reported to marriage and family therapists on a regular basis. There are as many varieties as there are people, but most in-law problems tend to fall into one of the following categories. You have an in-law challenge if your partner's parents:

- Treat you disrespectfully, ignore you, or are openly hostile
- Criticize you frequently in your presence, or to your partner
- Attempt to control you (and/or your partner) using money
- Attempt to control you (and/or your partner) using guilt
- Give unsolicited advice
- Attempt to drag you into family chaos caused by alcohol or drug abuse, fighting, or other ongoing personal issues
- Expect your partner to choose between you and them
- Expect your partner to meet their unmet emotional and/or practical needs

If any one of these issues is severe, it can disrupt your personal well-being and perhaps your marriage, too. If more than one dynamic is at work, it's important to take action to curb their potential negative impact.

The "Uncrossable" Boundaries

There are certain advisable boundaries that should be in place in your relationship to your in-laws. These are intended to ensure your well-being and protect your marriage (and children, if any) from the possible negative affects from problematic in-laws. Of course, there are individual differences and family styles, but in most cases these guidelines tend to protect everyone involved. Your in-laws should:

- Treat you with respect and courtesy
- Call or ask permission to enter your home
- Not interfere with your parenting values and rules
- Not make one of your children a favorite to the detriment of another
- Not expose you and your children to alcohol or drug abuse or violent or otherwise abusive behavior
- Not attempt to exclude you from family events
- Not interfere in your relationship with your partner

This last item is by far the most important and probably the hardest to enforce for all concerned. That's because this kind of behavior unfairly calls into question your partner's loyalty, potentially causing him to have to choose between you and his parents.

Putting Your Partner First in Decision Making

Say your partner's parents are very religious and they want you to raise your children in their church. While you may not observe any specific religious beliefs, you may not be comfortable with your in-law's religious preference. Whose comfort matters most here? The bottom line is clear: If pushed to choose, your partner must put you and your concerns first in the decision-making process around religious upbringing—or any other major decision about family values in your marriage.

Although clear and nonnegotiable, these issues can be difficult to manage. Parents can attempt to control adult children through monetary bribes, threats to remove inheritances, guilt, tantrums, or emotional exile. This same set of coercive, potentially divisive dynamics can apply in any number of areas of contention: where the two of you will live, how you'll decorate your home, how often you'll visit your in-laws, and, of course, how you'll raise your children.

And while all this may appear to occupy the grayest of gray areas, in actuality, it's black and white; your decision-making process gets to the basic premise of marriage and must be sacrosanct. In the case of religious choice, for example, on one hand you'd like to carry on family traditions, and you may agree that giving children a religious upbringing is preferable to none at all. However, if this choice is not agreeable to one of you, and the other proceeds with it to appease his parents, this will erode your marriage from that point onward.

Your Rights

In any marriage, there are certain rights and responsibilities reserved for you and your partner. Among these:

- The two of you alone must determine guidelines and agreements for the household you share
- You both alone will decide how to raise your children and how much access in-laws will have to the children
- You should expect your partner to put your (and the children's) needs first, above those of your in-laws
- You should expect to get his support for any problems you may have with your in-laws and to take a stand with his parents, if need be, to deal with those problems

Of course, you also have the obligation to keep any agreements you make with your in-laws, especially concerning loans or any other financial obligations. There's no more common source of conflict in families than money, especially when someone neglects to repay debts.

With Rights Come Obligations

As a daughter- or son-in-law you need to do your utmost to be gracious, open, and generous to your in-laws with your time and perhaps your home, too, and also offer emotional support when called upon. This is the sort of giving and receiving that is at the heart of what makes a family. There's an expectation that you'll go further and do more with one's family than you might for an unrelated acquaintance. However, setting the actual boundaries for what you will and won't do when it comes to your in-laws will always be an individual set of decisions—whether these decisions are openly acknowledged or not.

Planning Family Vacations and Holidays

A common area of contention between partners and in-laws concerns holidays and special family occasions. Families have traditions and sometimes in-laws are reluctant to embrace new ones or make room for changes to existing habits and rituals. One set of in-laws may take personal offense when an adult child chooses to celebrate Christmas or Thanksgiving holiday with his wife's in-laws. Suddenly you feel as if there's a competition between your parents and his, when all you may wish for is a little downtime on a holiday.

A common solution is to alternate holiday visits between two sets of in-laws. Or, you may wish to invite one or both sides of the family to your home for a holiday. Some couples try to eliminate potential friction by setting these alternating holiday responsibilities in stone, removing any room for competition or last-minute differences of opinion. Trial and error is often the best approach for new marriages. Whatever works for both of you must be the bottom line.

Solutions for In-Law Problems

Some bothersome behaviors can be ignored or laughed at; in fact, sometimes humor can be a highly effective tactic in dealing with problematic in-laws. To an interfering mother-in-law who insists on telling you a thousand and one better ways to make her son happy, you might say: "I really wish I was Mother Teresa, but unfortunately I'm not; in the meantime he'll have to deal with a mere mortal." The other possibilities—the in-law is unaware of the negative impact of her behavior on you, the parent is overly needy or meddlesome because of some lack in his own life, or your in-laws simply doesn't approve of you and want to drive a wedge between you and him— other tactics are called for.

The best way to approach the problem is directly. If you believe an in-law is unaware of her behavior, or its affect on you, a gentle boundary-setting move may be called for on your part. It may just be sufficient to say, "Your criticism of my cooking is really hurtful, could you please stop it?" Another way to handle it is to give her choices. "From now on, if you don't like my cooking, you can cook all the meals when we get together, or we can go out to eat at your expense—but I prefer not listen to your complaints about my cooking."

Essential

When confronting an in-law with an issue of concern, use "I" statements not "You" statements. Say, "I feel hurt when . . ." or "I'm upset about. . . ." Do not say, "You are so insensitive . . ." or "You hate me . . ." even if you believe it to be true. Don't sound like a victim. Do have realistic expectations of the encounter. People don't change overnight, and they rarely change unless they have something at stake.

Oftentimes, if an in-law is critical of you, she will verbalize those criticisms indirectly to your partner. Or the in-law may attempt to enlist your partner's cooperation in excluding you from family events. One young wife complained that her mother-in-law constantly invited her husband, the woman's only son, to accompany her to dinner and on trips without inviting his wife. Out of obligation and guilt the son would not refuse, even if he and his wife had already made plans.

Whether critical, cutting, or exclusionary remarks are made in or outside of your presence, either situation puts your partner in the middle and unfairly forces him to choose between you and his parent. What can be done about this unfortunately common situation? First you must discuss the problem with your partner. He may not be fully aware of his parent's negative impact on you. Or he's well aware of it and reluctant to confront his parents for fear of hurting them, in which case he's unconsciously choosing to hurt you instead. Your choices are to accept the status quo or to negotiate with your partner to confront the problem.

 **Alert**

> Give your partner warning that you wish to speak with him about an in-law issue. Avoid at all costs starting the conversation with "We've got to talk. . . ." Ideally, say something like, "When is a good time for us to talk about an issue involving your mother?" If he says right then, be prepared to address the topic calmly and firmly.

When you do approach him with the problem, be sure to focus not on who's good or who's bad in the situation but on how your in-laws' behavior makes you feel, and how you believe it's hurting your marriage. When you negotiate with your partner in this situation, always remember that it is probably very difficult for him. If necessary, give him time to think about it further on his own. If the problem situation doesn't improve, the best way to handle a difficult in-law dynamic is to have your partner stand up to the parent and draw a boundary—a line in the sand.

To set a clearer boundary with a parent, he can say some form of the following:

- I do not like to listen to you criticize my wife regularly; please stop it or I'll have to limit my time with you
- My wife and I have decided to do [whatever it is] and I need you to stay out of our decision making

None of these actions necessarily results in a positive response from your in-laws. There may be emotional or physical distance created, temporarily or for the long term, between your partner and his parents. This is potentially very painful for him. Give him emotional support or space if he needs either, and let him tell you what he needs.

When you confront an in-law with a concern and she refuses to deal with the issue, she'll likely respond in one of four ways:

- Deny the problem
- Say you are the source of the problem
- Play the victim
- Go on the attack and find fault with you

If you know you're dealing with an emotionally unhealthy in-law, it's best to be prepared for one of these negative reactions and then do what you need to protect yourself from any further negativity. In some cases, you may decide to limit your contact with that family member, while agreeing to have your partner visit separately. These are difficult individual decisions with a host of considerations that differ for everyone.

Privacy as a Marital Vow

On one hand it feels natural to look to parents with whom you may feel emotionally close for advice on a problem in your marriage. Certainly, doing so occasionally is not necessarily troublesome. It only becomes negative if it's habitual behavior that threatens your basic marital privacy. Because the marital relationship, especially in the beginning, can be fragile, the safest general rule is to avoid inviting your parents into intimate aspects of your relationship with your partner unless they are very supportive of your marriage.

When you deliver frequent negative reports on a spouse to a parent—for example, if you tell your mother that your partner behaved rudely, spoke in a nasty manner to you or a child, or otherwise was not the ideal son-in-law, but then neglect to mention the fact that you and he cleared up the misunderstanding or otherwise fixed the problem—you leave a lasting doubt or concern in your mother's mind about him. Because she is always there for you, or will always take your side, there is a real temptation to use her as a source of emotional comfort in times of conflict with your partner. Don't do it.

 **Alert**

Resist the temptation to complain about your partner to your parent. You risk putting parent and partner in an emotional bind that will be hard to undo. This same dynamic frequently plays out with an adult sibling.

Couples need to be careful not to allow in-laws to separate them with gossip and judgments. The reason there are so many mother-in-law jokes is because too many express opinions that attempt to divide the couple. If a man's mother attempts to do this, the man will have to stand up to his mother and set boundaries that protect his marriage. The same is true for the wife with her mother or father.

Essential

Family is not always created by blood. There are many people who have created their own families from friends, associates, church and synagogue members, and service groups. Family is a feeling of trust, companionship, and identification with others. Whoever is there for you when you need them can be counted as family.

Why Every Marriage Needs a Community

Too many couples today feel isolated and alone, without the support of an extended family. The world can be a cold and unfriendly landscape. There are times when only your family will support you. Family is the bank of last resort. Family is the safe harbor in a storm. It may seem inconsequential that family gets together for traditional holidays. It may appear ordinary when family members spend idle days together socializing with food. However, these rituals are far more important. Emotionally, the members of the family are bonding and supporting each other. Without family support, humans feel lonely, isolated, and lost.

There are many nontraditional family groups that are incredibly strong, supportive, and loving. In fact, when traditional family breaks down, creating your own family from friends and associates can work well for many people. Some people have found that when biological family members are toxic and destructive, replacement family members can work well. Family needs to be accepting, nonjudgmental, and loving. If your original family is cruel and judgmental, creating an alternative is advisable. The point is that humans need family whether that family is by blood or by choice. In family people find support and emotional nurturing, and both are essential for life.

Chapter 15

Marriage Therapy

WORKING WITH A trained marriage therapist or counselor offers you and your partner a lifeline, not just in times of crisis, but also as a preventive measure to ensure your long-term marital success. When smart couples find their once brilliant love is tarnished, they recognize that a few sessions of focused marriage therapy can help restore it to its former glory. Successful in life, such couples know that fine-tuning their relationship pays enormous dividends. If there are children, these partners take their commitment to make the marriage work to an even higher level, and use therapy to sort out difficult family dynamics that can be confusing. To believe that a successful long-term marriage is free of sustained work and effort is unrealistic and even destructive.

The Purpose of Marriage Therapy

Like marriage itself, marriage therapy is a highly demanding and rigorous process. It can be extremely uncomfortable to let down habitual defenses and delve into your core wound, and then share that pain with your partner—all in front of someone you hardly know.

So, why do it? First, if your marriage is in crisis, marriage therapy is often the only way to cut through the layers of hurt, defensiveness, and hopelessness that have hardened in place of the love you once had. Second, because this level of exposure—along with a commitment to making necessary behavioral changes—brings personal growth, and that growth brings many rewards.

If you do the necessary work, you'll come to accept yourself, wounds and all. Then, you'll find new ways to heal it and the scars left behind that get in the way of you being fully present in your marriage and available to your partner. You'll also gain a new ability to express your needs and respond with clarity to the needs of another human being with whom you've chosen to create a life. Finally, you'll learn to live in greater peace and harmony both within yourself and with your partner so the two of you can fulfill your vows to stick it out no matter what life throws at you.

 Fact

Many couples enter marriage therapy in what can only be described as an emotional stalemate and a behavioral standoff, wherein the two partners are simply enduring in a relationship that has degenerated into a state of nearly perpetual conflict.

Go Together or Alone?

If there are repetitive problems in your marriage, it is definitely advantageous for both of you to enter therapy at the same time with the same marriage therapist. Better to put all your cards on the table honestly and openly and have a neutral third party help you find a way through the dilemma than to keep you stuck in your point of view. This requires both individuals in the relationship be open to the value of therapy. Quite often one party is opposed to therapy. Unfortunately, that is usually the man because he sees the therapist as someone appointed as the judge and jury rather than a neutral party who is simply there to help the couple find their own solutions to their problems.

A good therapist will help both individuals see what each can do to improve the relationship, rather than choose one side over another. A therapist can help you both understand what is going on underneath the surface of a conflict. Often, the actual cause of the argument is not initially understood, because the real issue is hidden from consciousness.

 Question

What is the role of the therapist in marriage counseling?
A good therapist represents the marriage, not one or the other partner in therapy, regardless of who did what. A therapist is like the referee in sports; he keeps the process moving without allowing conflict to steer it off course.

The Role of the Marriage Therapist

The act of inviting a therapist into the sacred space of your intimate relationship is a statement of trust that the therapist must handle as both a privilege and as the grave responsibility it is. It is only after he clearly conveys this attitude that the couple will be able to trust him; it is from that trust that solutions may emerge. This is the essence of psychotherapy.

Here, Stephen Martin offers his view of the marriage therapist's role.

One of the most troubling questions I encounter during the first session of therapy with a couple is "Should we work on our marriage rather than just ending it?" My answer is always the same. "I assume since you have taken the time to see me and discuss this question with a marriage therapist then the answer is 'yes.' Otherwise, you would be seeing a divorce lawyer."

Divorce often shows a lack of imagination about how to live in a committed relationship. The real feeling that exists behind a couple's statement that they wish to end their marriage often is, "We are exhausted by trying the same old patterns and encountering the same failure. Can you give us any new ideas how we can be different in this relationship?"

Now that is an excellent place to begin. So let's explore the possibilities. After twenty-five years of practicing marriage counseling, I have found that within thirty minutes of listening to a couple, I can usually see what needs to change in their marriage. Of course, after just thirty minutes, most couples are not ready to hear what I can see. They first want to complain, release their anger, and express their frustration. Then, perhaps, they're ready to hear what is needed to repair the damage. Marriage counseling is not rocket science. It involves a basic comprehension of couple dynamics and the skills to help the couple see what they need to do differently in order to heal their marriage.

Although marriage counseling is not a complicated process, marriage is the most complicated human relationship I know of. It's complicated because, in order for it to work, the modern marriage must be an equal relationship. If your relationship is not equal, it will breed a power struggle. When one spouse holds more power than the other, eventually the relationship must come unglued. The reason is simple. An imbalance in the distribution of power will create disrespect and passive-aggressive behavior. The more powerful spouse will disrespect the weaker one, and the weaker one's hostile feelings will be expressed in a passive-aggressive manner. This imbalance of power is at the heart of most marital problems. It affects the self-esteem of both individuals in the relationship and results in the one who is weaker sabotaging the one who is more powerful. Many marriages of this kind are held together by the negative use of power. For example, traditionally most men have the power over money, while most women have the power over sex. As a result, in marital therapy, sex and money are the two most disputed issues. But most declared problems are not the real problem. The couple must look beyond their money and sex issues to see the underlying power struggle. Until they see this deeper dynamic, they will go around in circles fighting and struggling, complaining and hurting each other, but never really knowing what is at the root of their problems. In my experience, most couples blind themselves to their real issues, preferring to fight about issues that are merely symptoms of these underlying issues.

Enter the competent marriage therapist. The therapist should see the underlying dynamic of a marriage and have the experience to guide the couple to heal their original wounds. Not getting to the bottom of the real issue is like the story of the princess and the pea under the mattress. No matter how many mattresses she placed on top of the original mattress, until the pea is found and removed, she will not be able to sleep. Good marriage therapy finds the pea under the mattresses and teaches the couple how to remove the disruptions that are causing their strife.

How Long Will It Take?

There is an ancient saying, "When the student is ready, the teacher shall appear." Miraculous change can occur if someone is truly ready to hear something. Some couples find that just one session of therapy is all it takes to redirect their relationship to more positive ground. This is not common, but it is possible. For most people, it takes more work. The average length of all therapies in the United States today is six sessions.

Therapy doesn't need to be a lifelong process. A married couple can get enormous insights and learn new skills from marriage therapy done over a three- to six-month time period. If you are seeing a therapist as an individual, this may occur once a week. If a family or couple is in therapy, twice a month usually works better. Many couples find they need a couple of weeks between therapy sessions to learn the new skills suggested in their sessions and to practice the new behaviors they need to adopt to be more effective with their relationship. Like everything in life, the time required for change is unpredictable and unknowable. The time spent in therapy can be anywhere from one session to several years. Ultimately, you must make the informed decision.

Years may go by between your appointments with a marriage therapist, but once you have established a good relationship with that therapist, going in for a mental and emotional tune-up whenever the need arises can be a good idea. If married, a marital tune-up is very helpful. And these sessions should not go on and on, as you can be making the problem worse if you examine it in too much detail.

Finding the Right Marriage Therapist

The most critical part of the therapy process is a good, open relationship between client and therapist. It is the most significant predictor for success in therapy. People are different, and one therapist will be good for one person but ineffective with another. One session with a therapist should be enough to know whether she is the right therapist for you.

 **Alert**

If you don't feel good about your first session of therapy, don't return. You're in charge of the process, not the therapist. On the other hand, the role of a therapist is not to be your friend. If you find a therapist who always agrees with you, rather than one who asks you challenging questions and helps you examine your habitual thinking and behavior, that is a sign you may need a new therapist.

The goal of therapy is to help you find a new way to view a situation or person you find difficult, and from this enlarged perspective, discover a new response. Beware of any therapy that is not what you would describe as hard work. If it's too easy, you are not getting into the issues that need to be addressed. Unlike the emotional support you might get from telling your problems to a friend (or bartender, or hairdresser), therapy should not be about simply listening and agreeing with you.

 Question

What is meant by a level playing field in marriage therapy?
When a couple goes to marriage therapy, both partners must feel comfortable with the therapist or the process will not work well. Neither of you should feel that the other is getting preferable treatment, or that his concerns matter less. Neither is it the therapist's job to place blame on either of you for a problem in the marriage.

Don't misunderstand. You may not like what you hear, and that might be the perfect reason to stay with that therapist. However, if you do not feel your therapist understands what you are saying, or is not interested in you, or is emotionally vacant, or does not give you enough feedback, then find another therapist.

When to Bring the Children into Therapy

The question often arises, "Should children be a part of therapy if their parents are in great strife or when the marriage may be in the process of dissolving?" This is a difficult issue as the children are obviously affected by the couple's problems and the possible breakup of the family unit. Normally if the couple is having emotional tension, children should be shielded from the marital problems, but if the marriage is in the process of dissolving and is going to end in divorce, family therapy might be necessary.

The main key to consider is the age of the children. Unless the children are in their teens, it is best to shield the children from marital stress as much as possible. As the parent you should only answer questions they ask, and then keep your answers brief and simple. The best explanation to give children is that their parents, like all people, are having a tough time getting along right now and need outside help to resolve their problems, thus they are seeking professional help for their marriage. Make this a positive for the children. It can teach them that when problems occur, it is appropriate to seek professional guidance just as one seeks a dentist when there's a toothache, or a doctor for physical illness. If the results of the counseling are that a divorce is coming, the children have to be told at some time, and in an appropriate manner.

Generally, it's best to keep as much private in the marriage as possible, but this is not always possible. If the children see repeating or worsening tension in the marriage, they are involved. If they are involved, consider the best way to help them deal with what they are witnessing. If the tensions are severe and the children are old enough, a separate therapist to focus on the children's emotional needs may be advisable. This issue is addressed further in Chapter 18.

How Individual Therapy Helps a Troubled Marriage

Therapists are often asked, "I'm having trouble in my marriage, should I seek individual psychotherapy without my partner, or should we wait and seek counseling together?" The answer depends upon the nature of the difficulty and the willingness of both parties to seek the services of a marriage therapist. If your partner does not want counseling, and you are having trouble with your marriage, much good can come from individual sessions. Many people fear that if one party goes into marriage counseling alone, the result will be a divorce. That is definitely not the case. Most people who seek marriage counseling are looking for solutions to marital problems, not looking for a divorce. If a divorce is the intent, one party will find an attorney, not a marriage counselor. By its very nature, therapy asks the question, "What am I doing that I can change that will improve the situation?" Therapy is not about sympathy and passing blame upon others. It is always about taking control of your life and changing the only person you can change: yourself.

Essential

Seeking individual counseling about a marriage problem is not an admission that you are the problem; rather it is an attempt to find out how you can interact with your partner to decrease tension and resolve difficulties. It is an inquiry in how you might act so that your marriage will be better for both of you.

What can come from individual counseling for a couple's problems? By one person changing his approach in the relationship, he *can* change the marriage for both. In short, one person can make a difference. While eventually both must change for the problem to be completely resolved, one of the partners can produce a substantial change—enough to greatly improve the relationship—just by changing his own behavior.

Not exploring this possibility in individual therapy if your partner does not want counseling would be underestimating "the power of one" to act as a transformational agent. If your partner is not ready for counseling when you are, it's best that you take action and go to therapy alone, especially if the alternative is letting a problem fester. If you are looking for ideas that could change the internal dynamics of the relationship, exploration in individual therapy can provide valuable insights and offer approaches that you may not have considered. Many people incorrectly believe that change can only come through dialogue. Endless talking about problems does not solve anything. Action is the key to change. In individual therapy, you can discover and even role-play new dynamics that might help get the relationship unstuck in one or more areas. In this way, one person changing her behavior can be an effective strategy.

However, there is a danger in individual counseling for a marital problem that you need to be aware of. The therapist, being human, may side with you and reinforce your position in the disagreements, rather than searching for mutual solutions to the couple's problems. This could be a problem if the therapist becomes judgmental and becomes set in how he believes you should create a solution to the problems within your relationship. In summary, exploration of how you can shift the energy within your marriage is achievable in both individual and couples therapy. To deny yourself the opportunity to seek individual help if your partner doesn't want counseling as a couple is not only shortsighted but also could keep you stuck in difficulties for years while you wait for your partner to join you in working on the problem.

Remember, "the power of one" has been proven over time to be the deciding difference in making important changes in society. If it is true on a global scale, just imagine how much power you may have to make positive change within your relationship. So if you are experiencing difficulty in your relationship, ask yourself whether you should look into individual counseling or couples counseling.

 Fact

Individual counseling can be very supportive for the individual having difficulties in relationship and can help point out mistakes and perhaps even give you a better approach to take when dealing with a relationship problem.

Individual counseling can and often does make a relationship better. However, there are differences between individual and couples therapy. Both have their place and both hold value. Choose wisely, and do not be afraid to find another therapist if the one you are seeing is not working for you.

What Marriage Therapy Can't Do

Marriage therapy can only work if both individuals want to save the marriage. If one of the parties is determined to divorce, marriage counseling to stop the divorce is useless and is more likely to indicate that the other partner is in a state of denial about the disintegration of the relationship. Most marriages end because one of the partners has come to the conclusion that he would be happier living apart. Rarely do both parties agree at the same time that a divorce is right. The result is that the one being left will feel like the victim and have anger to deal with, while the one leaving will carry the guilt.

E ssential

Happy marriages have all the timing and grace of a trapeze artist. If you want to have such a relationship, you will have to work at it. Not just when you are in trouble, but before the magic wears thin. You will have to learn new skills and then practice these skills with all the dedication and finesse of the most agile, dedicated performers of the circus.

Marriage counseling is about teaching couples new skills to get along as a couple. What cannot be taught in marriage counseling is how to love another person and how to be committed to that person. Once one has fallen out of love, or has decided he wants the marriage to end, marriage counseling will not help. What it can do is help the reluctant partner come to terms with what is happening and limit the emotional damage done during a divorce. No counseling can talk someone into being in love with another. No counseling can teach commitment to another human being. No marriage counseling can hold together a marriage if one partner is determined to end it.

A generation ago, it was nearly always the female who brought her male partner into marital counseling to try to get things to change. The man usually sat silently with hostile body language while his wife spoke about their problems. His reluctance to be present, his silence and hostility to the entire process made counseling very challenging. His attitude, of course, had to be addressed before any progress could be made.

 Question

Who is the client in marriage therapy?
Contrary to conventional thinking, it's not the husband or the wife. It's not even the couple. The client is your marriage. You want and need your marriage therapist to be on the side of helping you to preserve and strengthen your marriage.

Today many more men initiate counseling for marital problems than in the past. While many people in past generations considered going for marital counseling a source of shame, that attitude has also faded with time. Marital intervention, whether help comes from a psychotherapist, a social worker, or an experienced religious counselor, is now a widely accepted and effective approach to finding solutions when your marriage is in trouble.

Chapter 16

The Newly Married Couple

STEVE AND MARIE entered marriage therapy barely a year after their lavish wedding—a three-day affair that cost more than a hundred thousand dollars. Nothing was spared for the couple's nuptials. Now, the young husband and wife were in a marriage therapist's office, broke and at each other's throats. So, what went wrong? First, with all the money spent on the wedding, not one cent had gone to premarital counseling. When the first signs of trouble arrived—not surprisingly, money problems—Steve and Marie blamed each other for overspending instead of facing their financial shortfall as a team. Their marriage had gotten off to a very poor start. Unfortunately, theirs is not an unusual predicament.

From Honeymoon to Hibernation

The first year of marriage is a notoriously difficult one, which is why it's so critical to know what to expect and how to deal with the problems that may arise. The first way to get off to a good start is to dedicate the first six to twelve months of marriage to the two of you, period. Think of it as a period of conscious hibernation away from family, friends, or any unnecessary distractions from the task of relationship-building. Like the grizzly bear in winter who climbs into a cave and stores food and energy for the busy months ahead, you and your partner need to store up on intimacy and communication, the essential building blocks of a long-term committed marriage.

At the end of this first year, your new marriage will be established, although still fragile, and the two of you should continue to treat it that way for another two years. This is true even if you and your partner were "together" several years before marrying. Marriage is different; ask anyone who's ever been married.

Too often newly married couples believe, and act as if, the skills required for a successful marriage come naturally and require no extra effort on their parts to acquire and refine. Not true! This is the time to work the hardest to get your marriage off on the right foot. Many marriages start to fall apart at three years. This is when disillusionment sets in after trial and error fails.

To avoid this outcome, you can read books about developing relationship skills (a suggested reading list is provided in Appendix B) and take couples communication workshops together. Practice what you learn at home. Be conscious of what you're creating. It will be with you for a long time. It's not unlike building the foundation of a house; it's a lot harder when you have to dismantle something first, rather than laying the first bricks and beams on cleared and ready ground. This doesn't mean your first year will not be fabulously fun, too.

The Importance of Sex

What will you do during all of this time alone as a couple? Perhaps it goes without saying, but if you're at all typical you'll have lots of sex. As young (or young at heart) men and women still in the first blush of romantic love, you and your partner have the opportunity to establish a rich and satisfying intimacy. You'll explore each other using all your senses. Ideally, you'll feel safe enough to ask for what you want, sexually and emotionally. Besides the pure ecstatic pleasure of satisfying sexuality, the best thing about all these uninterrupted hours in bed together is the opportunity to let down any walls that were in place when you felt you had to win each other over. If one of you isn't feeling sexually satisfied, broach the subject with your partner early, and gently suggest new things—before anything is set in stone. Within and beyond sexuality, now is the time to begin the lifelong process of being witnesses to each other's joys, sorrows, hopes, and dreams. Now is also the time to build the emotional intimacy that will hold your marriage together when the winds of change bring trouble into your lives.

Keep It Simple

For all the reasons given and more, this is the time to cement your relationship without the huge additional stresses of a newborn child. Unless you are facing a biological clock, or children or stepchildren come with the package, in which case you'll adapt and do your best, your chances of making your marriage work will be exponentially increased if you wait a year or even two before adding a third member to your new household.

 Fact

In a survey of causes for changes in marital satisfaction, of the men interviewed there was an average 67 percent drop in marital satisfaction after the birth of a first baby. The cause, according to the males interviewed, was a profound change in the woman. Common responses included, "I was no longer her priority" and "Her values changed."

As covered in depth in Chapter 12, a baby changes a woman's body for a year and more—taking into account pregnancy, nursing, and all those sleepless nights. An infant also supplants all or much of the attention and affection a wife previously reserved for her husband. This is a natural phase of motherhood but an often-challenging period in a new marriage. If at all possible, give your marriage a chance to find a solid footing before you add this challenge to your agenda.

Pitfalls of the First Year

Since you are unlikely to be spared these moments of crisis during your first year of marriage, it's better to think of them as the necessary rites of passage for any long-term committed relationship, rather than a cause of fear or dread. It's much better to be aware that they're coming so you'll not be surprised or thrown when the tough moments show up—especially since escaping the drama and difficult emotions that accompany these typical crises is just not possible.

There are eight typical pitfalls of the first year of marriage:

1. Different housekeeping styles: one slob + one neatnik = trouble
2. Your realization that each of you has at least one nasty habit or character flaw you weren't aware of before
3. Your first serious differences over money: one spendthrift + one miser = more trouble
4. Differences around sex, concerning either quantity or quality or both
5. Tensions around relationships with friends and/or family, including in-laws and stepchildren
6. Your first experience of "boredom" as a couple, sometimes accompanied by the first experience of straying, or the temptation to do so
7. Your first serious fight where one or both of you fights dirty (name calling, screaming, ultimatums, criticizing in public)
8. Buyer's remorse, your first realization that the marriage was a terrible mistake

After getting to the last item on this list, you can see why most marriage therapists describe the first year of marriage as the toughest. It's when the romantic fantasy must become a workable, daily reality. It's where the rubber meets the road. If you're smart, it's also when you make up for any lack of preparation before marriage by learning as much as you can about how to make a real marriage work.

After all these warnings of things to avoid, there is one absolute "must do" to get your marriage off to a good start. Early on in the relationship, you must learn to express appreciation—for both the large and small things your partner does for you and on behalf of the marriage. Express appreciation in a heartfelt manner. Express it often. Leave little notes saying "Thanks, it meant so much to me that you . . . did the dishes last night, or bought milk on the way home." Say it with a kiss and a hug or just a smile. Whatever it is you're grateful for, say so! Just don't say "thank you" without meaning it. There is (practically) nothing one spouse won't do for the other when a sincere statement or gesture of appreciation is made afterward.

In addition to expressing your appreciation for the nice things she does, you should never pass up an opportunity to appreciate her accomplishments and the other praiseworthy things about her. When she gets a promotion or a raise, celebrate. When he scores his personal best golf score give him a high five. When she looks beautiful, tell her. When you know he's worked his butt off to build a new fence say how much easier it will be to keep track of the dog or the children or simply how nice it looks. One of the most wonderful benefits of marriage is the experience of having someone on your side at all times. Be there for each other, and side with each other. Be each other's cheerleader.

Setting Up House Together

An important first step in establishing your first married household (even if you've lived together before marrying) is to make clear joint agreements concerning finances, household management, time together versus time spent apart, and a host of other items that come now that you've legally and emotionally thrown your lot in together. You can review these areas covered in other chapters—for example, power sharing in Chapter 3, and money in Chapters 6 and 7—putting special attention on how to make mutually satisfactory choices, how to stick to them and still maintain flexibility as conditions in your lives change and evolve.

One common mistake newlyweds make is taking on too much debt in the form of a home mortgage or high rent before they're ready, or without planning ahead to a point in the near future when one income might go away. This brings immediate money pressures and makes for an even more difficult first year of marriage. If it's at all possible, stay well within your financial means and allow yourselves the time and lack of pressure that comes with keeping your overhead low.

Friends: His, Hers, and Ours

In addition to combining extended families and acquiring a new set of in-laws, you and your partner also need to sort out which friends remain his, or hers, and, from these two separate groups of friends and perhaps coworkers, which will combine and become "ours." Whereas some of this sorting no doubt went on during your courtship, now that you're married, the discussing, choosing, and negotiating will likely become more pressing. Of course, you may be one of the unusual couples who have this completely worked out. If not, just know it's a natural phase of the process of partnering with someone.

 Fact

Many young married couples especially find it extremely valuable to have regular contact with one or more same-sex friends. The proverbial night out with the guys or girls can be a huge boon for keeping your marriage healthy.

Before you can begin this sorting process, you must come to an agreement with your partner about how you will socialize after marriage. This relates to the fundamental issue addressed in Chapter

11. How much togetherness is enough for each of you? Most married individuals find it important to retain independent interests and friends, and thus give each other "time off" from being part of a couple. The question is degree. Some couples permit each other substantial separate lives, while others are comfortable with much less separateness. This may also change in the course of your marriage. When there are young children, naturally, your social opportunities will dwindle temporarily.

Surviving Your First Blow-Up

One positive difference your married status should bring to your relationship is the expectation that you'll work things out, rather than split up the first time the relationship takes a nasty turn. This is the basic definition of commitment. There's no way to get to the other side of tough disagreements if one or both of you is constantly worrying that his partner will drop out if and when the going gets tough. The relationship must provide a safe container within which conflicts can be resolved. As it turns out, there are different types and levels of commitment in modern marriages.

The Deeper Meaning of Commitment

In her book *When Love Dies: The Process of Marital Disaffection*, Karen Kayser, MSW, PhD, offers a fascinating analysis of two decades of social science research done on marital commitment. She begins by distinguishing between people who hold an "institutional commitment" to marriage—that is, to the institution of marriage as a lifelong choice—versus those with a "voluntary or personal commitment," meaning two partners who believe in the institution but stay together only if they experience sufficient personal happiness or satisfaction within their marriage. Thus, this latter group makes a commitment to a person not an institution.

The author fashions her analysis with the starting hypothesis that those making voluntary commitments would be more satisfied because they work more consciously to keep their marriages satisfactory. However, the evidence proved otherwise. When Kayser correlates marital satisfaction with partners who fall into each category, she finds that a voluntary commitment is a strong positive indicator for marital disaffection or dissatisfaction. Conversely, those who regard their marriage as an indissolvable lifelong contract have a lower level of marital disaffection, and a greater level of satisfaction. Among the explanations offered for this difference offered in the research Kayser surveys are the possibilities that those with voluntary commitments to marriage have higher expectations of the marriage relationship and are then unwilling to accept less, and that persons of each type simply unconsciously select partners of the same persuasion (those more or less willing to trust and be faithful) thus reflecting their own belief system, and assuring a particular outcome. Kayser makes the salient observation that those married partners who make a voluntary commitment can fall into the predicament where the marriage (and the partner) must prove itself on nearly a daily basis.

Essential

Fights are inevitable and necessary in marriage, but if the marriage is to survive, they must be fair. The first time you allow yourselves to "fight dirty" it may be the beginning of the end of your marriage. It's a good idea to review the Ten Rules of Fair Fighting presented in depth in Chapter 5.

The most useful aspect of this area of social research for all married partners may be the spotlight it throws on the multiple definitions of commitment and the importance of knowing exactly what you and your partner are vowing to each other when you marry. Are you committing to the institution of marriage as much or less than to the person you're marrying? What if the person changes in the course of a decade or two of marriage? How can you avoid the trap of constantly assessing the value of your marriage, and run the risk of preventing the deepening of the relationship? These are critically important questions to consider before or at the beginning of your marriage. For most people, a true marital commitment can only occur if a vow is made—barring instances of abuse—as a definite "yes," rather than as a conditional, hypothetical "maybe."

Building a Strong Foundation

If marriage therapists were surveyed on the question of whether pre-marital counseling should be a requirement prior to granting marriage licenses—just as the department of motor vehicles requires training behind the wheel before issuing a driver's license and animal shelters make sure pet owners know how to care for a dog or cat before permitting adoptions—there's no doubt that 100 percent of therapists would vote "yes."

 Fact

Once you accept that marriages are from time to time hard work, finding new ways to deal with the problems you cannot resolve by yourselves is the purpose of marital counseling. The therapist brings new ideas and fresh prospective to the problems. If you do not get new ideas or fresh approaches from your marriage counselor, perhaps you need to find a new therapist.

Unfortunately, premarital education isn't a prerequisite to marriage, and divorce statistics remain abysmally high. All marriages have difficult times. It's safe to say that in 99 percent of marriages one or both partners have at some time considered divorce or separation as a solution to the stress all married partners go through. Considering divorce or separation is not strange or unusual. In fact, the opposite is true. It is unusual for married couples not to contemplate breaking up when tough issues seem irresolvable.

The larger point of concern is that many couples—who marry at many different ages—get all the way to the altar without probing very far into each other's hearts and minds, and without knowing enough about what love was, and wasn't. Neither do many couples have the required skills to get past those scary moments when love disappears and hatred takes its place. In short, they don't know how to make their marriage happy.

There is no more important time to get professional help than during the first year of marriage. This is the time to establish your marital agreements about money, children, household management, and your future goals together. This is also the time to tune up your communication skills and share the most intimate parts of yourselves with each other, including your core wounds and any lasting hurts you carry forward into adulthood, as well as your hopes and dreams. This is critical information for you to know about yourself—and your partner—if you are going to work together as a team and create the kind of lives you envision as committed partners. Then, as time passes, you will need new approaches to keep your marriage invigorated. You must embrace change, and you must keep communicating about each and every change, paying special attention to making the transitions in your marriage smooth.

Chapter 17

Marrying Different Cultures

TWO DIFFERENT RACES, cultures, or religions under one roof add to the often-noted fireworks created by matrimony. According to the 2000 census, 4.9 percent of married couples in the United States represented "mixed races." That's up from .7 percent in 1970. This huge increase in mixed marriages doesn't do away with many of the common problems that come up in today's multicultural marriage. If you are married to someone of a different race, religion, or ethnic group, your challenges arise from the different definitions each of you, and your respective in-laws, may have for what constitutes "normal" in a variety of situations. However, when you manage your differences well, you are also the recipient of many rewards.

The Challenges of Multicultural Marriages

The differences and potential conflicts in a multicultural relationship begin well before you get to the altar, and can remain present throughout your marriage. Perhaps one of you grew up with dinner conversations that were habitually loud and argumentative, while your partner was raised in an atmosphere where dinners were silent, reserved affairs. Perhaps his parents consider it appropriate to have a say in the most intimate decisions the two of you make—when and how many children to have, where you'll live, how you'll spend your weekends and holidays—an expectation that horrifies you as the more independent-thinking spouse. In a multicultural marriage, you are not just uniting two individuals; you're bringing together two different worldviews.

As a result, these marriages often require more care and communication compared to marriages where two people come from a similar background. The problems in multicultural marriages often concern these areas:

- The amount of contact you'll have with in-laws
- Sex role differences as related to work outside the home, housework, parenting, and socializing
- How far recent immigrants will assimilate into American culture, or retain ancestral cultural traditions
- The issue of racism or (the lack of) an awareness of bigotry shown by others in or outside the family
- Cultural expressions, including emotional displays, languages spoken, and relationships to elders or ancestors

Each of these topics can be loaded with tensions, so decisions about them require high levels of creativity and compromise between you and your partner.

In his book *Mixed Matches*, psychologist Joel Crohn describes three different approaches couples take when sorting out these choices:

1. One partner converts to the other's religion or cultural tradition
2. Both partners transcend their respective cultures or faiths and choose a new religion or choose a nonreligious secular or assimilated cultural path
3. The two partners create a balance of two cultural traditions, drawing on aspects of both

Each of these approaches might work better in your marriage. One note of caution Crohn offers: Some couples find that if they replace an active religious or ethnic lifestyle with a wholly secular way of life, they risk a loss of meaning or community. The importance of tradition, family rituals, and spiritual life should not be underestimated for you and any children you may have now or in the future.

When Different Religions Marry

In some religious traditions where marriages are still arranged, making a so-called love match is an issue of contention for parents and adult children. In conservative or fundamentalist branches of Christianity, Judaism, and Islam, males and females socialize, worship, and learn separate from each other. Within the same families, certain members are lax or lapsed in their religious observances, while others follow strict rules for holidays, meals, and dress, among other things. The areas for conflict are ripe when you're encountering so many differences.

If you are marrying or are already married to someone of another religion, you may be aware of the potential land mines. For example, there's the decision to wed by a priest or in front of a rabbi. If you or your partner is Jewish, the issue of whether to circumcise a newborn boy, or not, can be hugely important. There is also the question of whether or not to baptize, which is a must in observant Catholic and conservative Christian families. As much as possible, it is best for the two of you to address the resulting issues and choices prior to or early in your marriage. In this vein, it's important to look inside you and within your extended families to confront any religious prejudice that may be there, consciously or not. If prejudice arises in relation to your partner or his family, it is best to confront it immediately, and set boundaries for what is acceptable when dealing with each side of the family.

When sharp religious or cultural differences are present, you need to realize that mutual understanding and full acceptance may take time. Do not attempt to be more knowledgeable than you really are about another religion, and do not attempt to sound politically correct at the risk of being honest about your feelings or needs. You may, out of courtesy and respect, don a scarf to cover your head when entering a mosque or traditional Christian church, but that doesn't mean you are likely to trade in your basic values in exchange for another's.

Essential

Many more members of different faiths are intermarrying, up to a fivefold increase from the 1950s to the 1990s, representing an estimated 33 million Americans now in such intermarriages. In each of the following faiths, the percentage of those who've married outside their religion are: 21 percent of Catholics, 32 percent of Jews, 30 percent of Mormons, 25 percent of Lutherans, and 40 percent of Muslims.

Planning Holidays and Special Occasions

Parents and grandparents of today's intermarried couples tend to hold to more traditional customs than do their younger, more culturally assimilated adult children. This makes the use of greater sensitivity when planning for holidays with your multicultural extended family very important as a daughter- or son-in-law. Even within your marriage, when you and your partner come from very different backgrounds there is no single standard of "normal" or "customary" available to apply to holidays or other special occasions. Because of this reality, you may wish to alternate holiday observances between your two traditions, or select one set of traditions, or create your own.

Throughout this process of coming to terms with ethnic or religious differences, it's vital to understand the role of ritual and ceremony in your lives. Without the marking of milestones, whether a birthday, anniversary, graduation, or even the New Year, it's easy to feel adrift and become alienated, caught up in the stress of life without the grounding influences ritual and ceremony can provide. And so, if your spouse's family observes a Chinese New Year, unless the two of you have made a clear decision in another direction, it behooves you to mark this date on your calendar and do something to honor the occasion. You and your children will only be enriched by this inclusion.

 Fact

Second- and third-generation immigrants intermarry at much higher rates than their parents. For example, 31 percent of U.S.-raised Asian American males married white Caucasians, and 36 percent of Asian American females did so—compared to 5 percent or fewer of the members of their parents' or grandparents' generations who married outside their race or Asian culture.

There is always an enormous amount that someone from one culture or religion doesn't understand about someone else's. This ignorance can be based on intolerance, but more often the problem is the outsider's feeling of embarrassment about asking questions or seeking inclusion. The right approach when you come into a new culture is to be willing to ask, listen, and, where appropriate, be willing to experiment with the other person's cultural traditions and rituals.

Nuts and Bolts of Cultural Differences

Would you like wine with dinner? While this question is not controversial in most settings, in a Muslim culture, it can be seen as insensitive, even insulting. How about midday naps? In certain cultures they're customary, while in others, the average person would deem a healthy adult who leaves work to nap at noon as lazy or irresponsible. Do you feel comfortable making personal decisions as a large extended family group, or do you prefer to keep matters just between you and your partner? These issues are evidence of cultural roots in one place or another or one religion or another. How you put them together can make or break your marriage.

E ssential

Things not said and divisive issues prompted by cultural differences don't simply go away; they fester and erode your marriage. To have a healthy marriage, you must say how you feel and what you need in order to feel safe, loved, and respected in your home and also when you're in the presence of extended family.

The first step to do this in a positive, creative manner is to identify your differences. Then learn as much as you can about each other's cultures, religions, or backgrounds. Where were your partner's grandparents born? How many generations have lived in America? Which relative was the first, if any have, to attend college? Who is the black sheep in your partner's family? What did he do to get that mantle?

A good rule of thumb is not to assume you understand aspects of another culture, or that you understand each other. Caution is best.

Language Barriers

Speaking multiple languages can be a benefit when it comes to living in a modern interdependent world and working in a global economy. However, at home and especially when dealing with in-laws conversant in different languages, communication and family cohesion can be adversely affected. It's natural for people to not go outside their comfort zones, but when the adults in marriages and extended families don't reach out across language barriers, they set a poor example for children.

At Stuart and Maria's wedding, her Spanish-speaking parents, siblings, and large extended family—including immigrants

and first-generation members from Puerto Rico—sat by them-
selves and interacted only minimally with Stuart's English-only
speaking relations. Little changed after this couple's wedding.
Throughout their marriage, even though the families lived
only a few miles apart, holiday observances and socializing
remained mostly separate, with Stuart's parents professing a
preference to keep it that way. This choice caused Maria, espe-
cially, great emotional distress. She blamed Stuart in part for
not taking a stronger stand with his parents, or learning Span-
ish so as to better communicate with her family. She wanted
their two children, ages five and seven, to feel a part of both
cultures, but she noticed that neither child wanted to learn or
speak Spanish with her family or away from home. Of course,
there were other issues in addition to different native tongues
serving as barriers in Stuart and Maria's extended family—
culture and class among them—but the issue of language, if
approached more cooperatively and creatively, might signifi-
cantly turn this unhappy marriage and in-law situation in a
more positive direction.

Anyone who travels to a non-English-speaking country knows
that if you make even a minimal effort to speak the native language,
you are immediately given a warmer, more appreciative welcome in
that country. The same can be said for intercultural marriages and
in-laws; a little effort goes a long way.

Raising Biracial or Multicultural Children

The good news has to do with the changes reflected in present and
future generations when it comes to multiculturalism in general
and biracial children in particular. In a world united by mass media,
especially evident in today's music, film, and Internet, kids increasingly think beyond the racial and ethnic barriers of the past.

This doesn't mean your biracial child will not encounter racism
or that your child of mixed cultural or religious heritage won't also

be sometimes met with prejudice, but it does offer hope and the reassurance in light of the quickly changing demographics of the United States, which point to the nation having a majority population that is multicultural and nonwhite by 2050.

 Fact

Today's under-thirty generation is much more open to biracial dating and intermarriage than their parents and grandparents. In one recent online survey of Gen Y attitudes, 91 percent said interracial dating is okay. More than one-fifth of Americans have a close relative married to someone of another race.

Issues may arise in your immediate family and have more impact on you as parents when your children are biracial or multicultural. A child may, as he matures, elect one or neither of his parents' religious faiths. He may choose to assimilate completely and eschew observances of any ethnic or religious flavor. These choices may be very difficult for you or your in-laws to accept. Compromise may or may not be possible, especially with an adolescent or young adult child. Acceptance is your best route as a parent.

Chapter 18

Divorce as Last Resort

MAKE NO MISTAKE about it; divorce is a profound emotional, financial, and spiritual disruption. Many men and women will say they consider a divorce to have been the worst experience of their lives. Usually, the spouse initiating a divorce carries the guilt, while the one not wanting the marriage to break up assumes the anger—and the role of victim. In reality, both spouses suffer enormously before, during, and after a divorce occurs. No one, not even a therapist, can tell someone if and when she should seek a divorce. In this chapter some reflections on divorce are offered in hopes of lending a new perspective to those facing this painful decision.

How the Idea of Divorce Functions in Marriage

Once upon a time, not so long ago, when a bride and groom stood at the altar and repeated the vow "Until death do us part," they meant it as a lifelong, unbreakable commitment. Divorce laws of the past reflected the vow's black-and-white meaning, and there were enormous social pressures to stay married. Now, for many, this notion of permanence seems quaint. Notwithstanding the historical inequities of traditional marriage and property laws that harmed women and children and required reform, it's time to acknowledge the unforeseen costs that came when the definition of marriage was transformed from a permanent to an impermanent union.

Increasingly, the idea of divorce (or the contemplation of divorce as an option) functions as the solution for personal unhappiness within marriage. It's also fair to say that divorce as an idea serves as a rationalization used by an unhappy spouse who chooses to give up on the commitment they made at the altar. Arguably, this revised concept of marriage as inherently impermanent, and the use of divorce as a solution for all things that go wrong in the marriage relationship, inflicts a sizeable amount of harm on the husband and wife and, especially, on the children who must face the real, lifelong consequences of the dissolution of the family they hold dear.

Fault and No-Fault

During the 1970s, divorce, and by extension the institution of marriage, went through a major transformation with the introduction of the legal concepts of no-fault divorce and community property. Prior to this time, fraud had to be publicly proven in a court of law in front of a judge who would then decide who was "at fault" in the marriage and whether or not to grant the divorce. He could then award custody and make financial dispensation of any and all marital assets. This system of divorce was costly and it produced shame, embarrassment, and often the public ridicule of an entire family. The burden of proving marital fraud in a courtroom became so acrimonious that these contested divorces tore many families irreparably asunder.

No-fault divorce allows two people to dissolve a marriage without any evidence of fraud, with the most common, often perfunctory legal reason for divorce now given as irreconcilable differences. In most states, after the impersonal processing of a few official documents, each divorced spouse walks away with half of the marital assets and her independence. At first this approach seemed humane as it reduced the disastrous affects associated with the public humiliation of divorce trials. However, it produced other challenging ramifications.

What now appears clear is that after divorce became legally easier and more socially acceptable many people didn't include the idea of "till death do us a part" in their thinking about the marriage vow. They may have said the same words, but either didn't take them seriously or didn't think through their implications, leaving millions of husbands and wives psychologically unprepared for the difficult times all marriages bring.

 Fact

According to the National Center Health Statistics, America's divorce rate began rising in the late 1960s and jumped during the 1970s and early 1980s, as nearly every state enacted no-fault divorce laws. The rate peaked in 1981 at 5.3 divorces per 1,000 people. Since then it has dropped by one-third.

It seems that at least half of those who stood at the altar and spoke the words "Until death do us part" meant instead, "Until this gets too hard," or "until I get bored with you and someone better comes along." This is not to say that the millions of people who married and divorced over the past three decades were being dishonest or deceptive while going through with those marriages and subsequent divorces. What is far more likely is that with the help of the larger culture many were deceiving themselves.

Women and Men in the Modern Divorce

Since the 1960s, women have been working in greater numbers and are thus less economically dependent upon men. During this same period, women have sought divorces much more frequently than ever before. The most recent data show that the majority of divorces today are initiated by the female, and, according to a 2004 survey by AARP, after age forty, the number jumps to two-thirds. While economic and legal changes have allowed more women to consider divorce, there are other, strictly emotional dynamics that may be pushing more women from simply considering taking this step to going through with it.

Women have a deeper sense of what is possible in an emotional relationship, and with greater independence many are less willing to tolerate inadequate, emotionally unsatisfying marital relationships. Men on the other hand seem generally more content in marriage especially if they are physically cared for by the female whom many have unconsciously come to relate to as mother replacements. Also, in many cases men who are unfamiliar with feelings—now called having a low emotional intelligence—permit the female to carry the emotions for both of them, a burden that can become very difficult for the woman in a marriage.

At the most simplistic level, one which women often find offensive, many men tend to see marriage as an exchange of services. They take out the garbage, take care of the cars, and mow the lawn, while the woman tends to the inside of the house, offers sex, and takes care of the children. For these men, this set up feels like an equal exchange, while women tend to see this as too much giving on their part and not enough receiving.

When June and Stan came into therapy, June summed up the problem in the marriage in these strikingly simply words. "There's just too much giving and not enough getting." June and Stan were in their forties, had three school-age kids, and both worked full time, yet June felt the burden of the housework and caring for the children. As the unconscious assumptions of this relationship were further exposed, it appeared that, at first, June gave these gifts to Stan without resentment, and he was only too happy to receive them. With the passage of time, June began resenting the imbalance and, as her resentment grew, she began to close down emotionally toward Stan. With this emotional shutdown, their physical intimacy ceased, and Stan began to store up resentment toward June for withholding sex.

This is the stalemate June and Stan had reached when they began marriage therapy. And this is exactly how the marriage would have stayed if June had not issued an ultimatum to Stan. "Come with me to marriage therapy or I'm leaving you and taking the kids."

Stan, who professed to having had "some awareness" of the problems in the relationship but figured "they were normal in long-term marriage," had to be shocked into seeing the problems as serious enough to threaten the marriage. Since Stan did not want a divorce, June's decree that they either enter therapy or separate worked to move the relationship toward healing.

The process of marriage therapy eventually helped Stan realize that the shutting down of sex in the marriage was his responsibility as much as June's. Stan learned this only after the two had some painful and revealing exchanges. With encouragement June made the "I" statement, "I need to be touched without immediately having intercourse," and then explaining that she craved emotional satisfaction and without it, she could no longer open up to Stan sexually. In order for Stan to hear her, June had to move past her anger and reveal the hurt she felt underneath. Although confused at first, Stan eventually became emotional too, saying, "I'm sorry, I just didn't get it. The last thing I want to do is starve you or hurt you."

Slowly Stan learned the even harder lesson of how to find and honor his own feelings, which allowed him to be more receptive to June's. As he became more knowledgeable about emotional connectedness, June became more available to Stan for sexual activity. She felt loved and reassured that Stan cared for her emotionally. With these changes the marriage began the healing process, with all the richness that is available when each takes responsibility for his own feelings and then opens up to care for his partner's, too.

Stan's ignorance of his internal emotional life is very common for males. Men often have to learn about emotional connectedness after they get married, while women understand these principles naturally. It's also true that some women feel too much; they can find themselves flooded with emotions. For a marriage to work harmoniously, this imbalance has to change. If each is aware of the need to rebalance heart and head within the relationship, a wife can teach her husband about emotional satisfaction, and a husband can teach his wife about controlling her emotions when it's necessary to do so. Many men tend to be dismissive of emotions in human beings, and this attitude can make a man unwisely see his wife's emotional display as manipulative and then harden himself toward her, which is the very thing you do not want to have happen if the marriage is going to improve.

The Reasons to Go Through with a Divorce

The decision to dissolve a marriage is extremely personal. While divorce is always a failure, sometimes it's a necessary one. Physical or emotional abuse is the main reason people should seek a divorce. Physical abuse is easy to assess, while emotional abuse is far more subjective. This type of abuse is just as real and can be severely damaging to its victims. Emotional abuse can include one spouse making degrading remarks, being very controlling, or emotionally neglecting the other spouse.

The addiction of one spouse is another extreme and potentially abusive situation. In cases where one partner is in the grips of an addition to a substance, or a behavior such as gambling or sex, and if she is refusing professional help for her addiction, separation or divorce may be necessary for the protection of the spouse and children. Many spouses dealing with an addicted partner find support and suggestions on how to help the addict and themselves from the Al Anon twelve-step program. Associated with Alcoholics Anonymous, these all-volunteer organizations are in every community (check your phone book) and offer their valuable services anonymously and free of charge.

Essential

If you are the victim of spousal abuse, your first job is to find a safe place for you and your children. Try to avoid painting the image of the other parent as a perpetrator. This can make a child distrust the sex of the offending parent. Where a mother has conditioned a daughter to see her father as "evil," she can grow up to view all men as "evil."

Before you make a decision to divorce your spouse, you should make at least one visit to a marriage and family therapist. Like the dentist who is trained to understand what is happening to your teeth, therapists are trained to understand the difficulties within a marriage and family. Seeking outside guidance before making such a large decision is obviously desirable, just as it is better to go to the dentist than take a pair of pliers to extract a tooth from your own mouth because it is painful.

When Just One Partner Wants a Divorce

If you feel the need to divorce your partner but he does not wish this to happen, your first step should be to reflect on whether you might be able to change your reactions to your partner's offensive behaviors. If you've tried and failed, then you must let your partner know exactly what is bothering you, and see if he can change the behavior. Often, the best way to try to effect such changes, particularly if communication between you has broken down, is through marriage therapy. Rushing into divorce is not the answer.

Better to pull out your own teeth with pliers than take on a divorce without outside guidance and counseling—especially when underage children are involved. Still, the majority of divorces occur without any sort of outside help, whether that help comes from a minister, rabbi, or licensed therapist.

 Fact

According to the NCHS, the divorce rate for people with higher levels of education has fallen slightly over the past decade, while the number of divorces for those without a college degree has stayed the same. Noted author on marriage, sociologist Stephanie Coontz, attributes this difference to education giving people better communication and negotiation skills—both essential for a marriage. Coontz also pointed to studies that show a wife's work outside the home tends to stabilize a marriage.

Revisiting "For the Sake of the Children"

Before the legal and social sea changes that fundamentally altered the institution of marriage in the 1970s, unhappy spouses stayed married "for the sake of the children." In the decades since, this view has often been derided and denied as unnecessary, even antiquated. However, as one out of two marriages end in divorce, up to one million children per year continue to experience the trauma of divorce. Only within the past ten years has it become brutally clear that the negative impact on divorce on these children has been disproportionate (compared to their parents) and dire.

One landmark study on the impact of divorce on adult children conducted by Judith Wallerstein caused major reverberations when it was released in 1999. In this study, Wallerstein and her colleagues resoundingly demonstrated that parental divorce causes heretofore unacknowledged emotional and behavioral negative consequences—including mood disorders, school failures, and relationship problems—in 25 percent of adult children of divorce who were tracked in many cases into their forties. This was compared to

10 percent of adult children from intact families who experienced these problems.

Wallerstein's study demolished a popular myth advocating the view that it is less harmful for children to experience the temporary trauma of divorce than to witness parents' ongoing marital unhappiness. In reality, the degree of damage to children depends upon the level of unhappiness or abuse they witness. A good case can also be made that when children witness divorce they are seeing a harmful example of their parents' failure to keep a lifelong commitment. Which is the worse behavior for a child to witness firsthand: marital conflict or the avoidance of commitment? Only you can decide, based on your own marriage and personal experience.

This all assumes underage children are involved in the marriage. When two adults without children come to such a volatile crossroads in a relationship, the bar is obviously much lower. Personal growth can be valid reason for a divorce when one of the parties believes he has worked extremely hard to bring improvement to a marital relationship and is frustrated by a lack of effort by his spouse or a lack of results. If children under eighteen are involved in your decision, the decision should be examined with much more care and concern for the children's welfare.

Creative Solutions for the Sake of the Children

If there are underage children involved, perhaps other arrangements can be made so the marriage can continue until the youngest child reaches eighteen. You may be able to remain husband and wife and parent your children while maintaining quasi-independent lives. One of you may have an additional residence. Remember there are no longer any or many hard-and-fast rules for marriage. The man and woman in each marital relationship independently create most of the rules that govern their lives together.

Within the realm of what's considered acceptable in modern-day America there are many flavors of marriage; there are commuter marriages where couples reunite monthly, marriages with stay-at-home dads, same-sex marriages, marriages where exes share holidays together with a new spouse and all their children, and many other creatively structured relationships where the central objective is to sacrifice or adjust adult needs to meet the primary needs of the children—whether these are social, emotional, financial, or all of the above. Seeking outside therapy can assist you in finding other ways to remain in the relationship for the purpose of keeping your family intact until the children are older.

Essential

Before you make the decision to have a child with your partner, take the necessary time to consider—and discuss in depth—whether both of you can imagine this marriage lasting for the next eighteen years. This is not an easy conversation for any couple to have. Arguably, though, you owe it to your children to endure that discomfort to have a better chance of assuring their future well-being.

The completion of the commitment you made when you married and especially after you created a child together contains an integrity that is often overlooked—or worse, scorned as "old fashioned" —in today's individualistic culture. Once again, underage children are the real victims of a divorce. It is their well-being that must be considered before the decision to divorce is made final, or before a family is dissolved.

The Decision to Divorce

Sometimes, simple statements say it all. Like, every marriage has good and bad times. Many marriages don't make it through one year. A good number of others succumb at the aptly named "seven-year itch." If you were happy and relieved that your marriage made it through these familiar pressure points, but now find it very troubled, first be aware that you're probably not thinking clearly in this difficult time. Emotions, from hurt and anger to grief and fear, can be overwhelming. So how should you make the difficult emotional decision to divorce if you are currently weighing this possibility?

One deceptively simple method is to write out a list of the positive and negative aspects of your marriage and carefully weigh the pros and the cons. Put all the reasons for ending your marriage on one side of the page, and the reasons to stay married on the other side. Then attempt to give a weight or point value to each positive and negative point, from one to ten, so that you rationally see what the choices are and how important each is. Think hard about why you are ranking each as you are. The fact that your husband is a great father to your children might deserve a point value of ten and lead the "pro" column, while his inability to share his emotions may merit a six and go in the "con" column.

The idea of this exercise is to slow down the decision-making process behind a divorce.

 **Alert**

When considering a divorce, slow down the decision-making process. When divorce is frivolously chosen, your experience of commitment is shortchanged. It is a dangerous romantic fantasy to believe that a good marriage is an easy one, free of conflict. If you and your spouse don't know how to fight fair, this is a skill set that you can learn.

Are you and your marriage strong enough to withstand conflict? A good marriage provides a safe container for conflicts to be worked on and resolved. A marriage that looks calm and peaceful on the outside can be stagnant or even rage-filled on the inside. The only way to create this safe container is for both of you to make a rock-solid commitment to keep working at it—especially when the times get tough. It's not that divorce should be abandoned. Just because it is slowed down does not mean divorce should be or could be taken away as an option.

Trial Separations

Temporary separations can help a troubled marriage. The problems and the stress they cause can be mitigated with a little space from your togetherness. A separation can provide new insight into what is valuable and what cannot be tolerated in the marriage. Because people fear that a separation always ends in divorce, they may avoid it as an option, but many couples gain new vitality from spending some time apart from each other. Think of it as a trial divorce. Then you will better know what is best for you, your family, and your children. In Stephen Martin's twenty-eight-year marriage therapy practice, he estimates that half the couples who've tried trial separation got back together after six months.

A trial separation may also help expose the real, perhaps hidden issue underlying one partner's desire for a divorce. For example, an issue that frequently leads to divorce is the deep unhappiness within one of the partners in a marriage. Often, that unhappiness is self-created, but, while living with his wife, the one feeling unhappy cannot completely understand his reasons for it. By the point at which he is considering divorce, he could be projecting that unhappiness on his partner. He may believe that if he were no longer married to her, he would find happiness.

 Fact

Many people view trial separation as a euphemism for divorce. This is simply not the case. Often, time apart can help a troubled marriage—especially if one or both partners use this time to reflect and work on their individual issues.

Individual Therapy During a Trial Separation

If one partner feels extremely alienated, it's best for the one feeling deep unhappiness to spend some time living alone. While alone, he should seek individual therapy to see if the problem can be corrected within himself, thus making a divorce unnecessary. If, on the other hand, the problem is toxicity within the relationship, and he is convinced that the toxicity cannot change, try marriage therapy next, and, if all else fails, perhaps a divorce is the only reasonable alternative.

Review Chapter 15 to learn some of the benefits of individual therapy for a troubled marriage. When one partner doesn't have clear emotional boundaries, or doesn't have a good sense of his own feelings, individual therapy can quickly offer some remedial help by providing the one in need some skills that allow for a higher level of conflict resolution and thereby give the marriage another chance.

How to Inflict the Least Damage on Your Children

Divorce ends a marriage, but should it end a family? Everyone needs the safety and support of a family, and when it is torn apart by a divorce, the consequences can be disastrous. In order to minimize the damage to the children (should a divorce become necessary), conflict between Mom and Dad should be kept out of view from the rest of the family. The relationship between two married people is distinct from the relationship between a mother and a father of a family. Wise parents who need to divorce each other know that divorce does not end a family; they struggle to keep parental ties intact and continue working as a team to parent the children while they let go of their marriage.

To facilitate this, each parent should obviously refrain from telling the children her personal grievances with the other parent. Unfortunately this rarely happens as emotions spill over and, inside the emotional disruption that ensues, parents tend to complain about the other parent in front of the children. Immature parents either consciously or unconsciously wish to force the children to make choices between mother and a father. Nothing can disrupt a child's life more than siding with one parent over the other, and it's both immature and selfish for a parent to encourage this alienation between a child and his other parent. Children never want to choose. When this happens it inevitably is the result of either parent forcing this decision on the child, unless the children witness extreme abuse or neglect.

When telling children of a coming divorce it is best to have the child see her own therapist to handle the emotional disruption she is experiencing. Give as few details as you can, and only answer questions she asks. Attempt to have children remain nonjudgmental about the coming divorce. Teach them it is not their fault. Most children blame themselves when a divorce occurs. As irrational as it may seem to adults, most children of divorce are tortured with the notion that if only they had been better children, their parents would not need to split up. Whatever the situation in a family or stepfamily, divorce is never a child's fault; it is the failure of two adults to get along as husband and wife. Let your children know you will always be a father and a mother to them, that what is changing is simply the role of husband and wife. Again, the family is not divorcing; the husband and the wife are changing their roles inside the marriage, not inside their family.

After a Divorce

Once divorced, emotionally mature parents try to get along as parents and let their marriage go. This means your conversations as parents should (at first) be limited to just the children and their well-being. Sensible parents know that you never divorce a child, even if you have to divorce the child's other parent. The key to success in this difficult transition is making a distinction between your roles as husband and wife and your roles as father and mother. Healthy families navigate a divorce by understanding the different roles and never destroy the role of the other parent in the eyes of their children.

If you need to complain about your ex, never do it with the children. Find friends or seek professional guidance to grieve the loss of the marriage and release the anger of a divorce. Usually a divorce will take at least three years to heal from. Allow yourself the time to grieve, to feel angry, hurt, and disappointed, but keep this from your children. Children never want to choose between good parents . . . they always want their parents to get along and love each other. Sometimes it takes a divorce to accept and appreciate the other parent of your children. If you've tried many different approaches (including individual therapy, couples counseling, and a trial separation) to save the marriage and failed, perhaps the divorce was necessary. If that's the case, better to get along as Mom and Dad than hate each other as husband and wife.

Chapter 19

Making Remarriage Work

WHEREAS IN MANY areas of life failure leads to lessons learned and a greater chance of future success, this is often not the case in marriage where 60 percent of second marriages and 75 percent of third marriages eventually fail. With these stark side-by-side realities, it doesn't take much insight to conclude that people are not paying enough attention to learning new relationship skills between these marriages. There are at least two serious fault lines at work here. The first is not taking the time and effort to heal from your divorce, and, by extension, reflect on and change your own problematic behaviors that contributed to the downfall of the relationship. The second is having unrealistic expectations of your new marriage, to believe that it will make up for and replace all that was wrong in your previous marriage with all that is good and right.

Look Back and Learn

Learning from the past is essential if you wish to reprogram your thinking and change your behaviors from those that cause failure to new ones designed for relationship success. The way you use hindsight is what makes the difference. The practice of using hindsight to learn from the past is useful as long as you don't use it to attack yourself rather than as a way to learn and grow.

Too many people limit the self-examination they do between marriages to this "would have, could have, should have" syndrome. Rather than adjusting the present from the past, they look at prior mistakes and beat themselves up and do damage to their self-esteem. Worse, if you use the past in this way, you may be so busy being self-critical that you don't learn the important lessons lying right before your eyes. If you gently accept past mistakes and then make adjustments in the present, it can be positive.

When you experience a catastrophe you have a choice as to how you will respond to the event. You do not get any choice about the incident. It has already happened. Most people live their lives regretting events that have already happened. Nothing can take you back in time to reverse the facts, and thus living your life as a victim of the past is not wise. So, learn gently from the past, do some individual psychotherapy, but ultimately you need to trust yourself and don't get the "would have, could have, should have" syndrome. The only way to make a new marriage work is to accept the events and mistakes that have already occurred and embrace them as lessons and teachers.

How to Heal a Broken Heart

Nothing is as painful as a broken heart. Many people would say that physical pain is easy to handle compared to the emotional pain of a lost dream, such as a failed marriage or a split-up family. With physical pain, there are clear avenues for relief, but how do you heal a broken heart? The first rule is to feel all the difficult feelings. If you resist the feelings, or "stuff the emotion," the pain will stay around in the unconscious, hidden from your view, but it will not go away. It will emerge from time to time as anger, cynicism, or depression. Time heals, but only if you face the emotional pain and experience it with your mind and heart wide open.

Finally, it is important to understand the emotional process that occurs when your heart is broken and you've experienced a major loss. Through the pioneering death and dying work of

Elizabeth Kubler Ross, the five stages of grief were identified and explored.

Essential

Unwillingness to feel the pain of a broken heart is like nursing a broken bone without medical devices. Of course, bones heal without medical attention, but they may heal in a disjointed manner and cause lifelong disfigurement. Even the toughest athlete will get medical attention for a broken bone, but far too many people still believe they can emotionally heal without assistance.

Here are the five stages of grief, revisited and applied to divorce and remarriage:

1. **First comes denial.** In this stage, you cannot accept what happened to you and to your marriage, so you deny the truth, hoping that in denial the experience will somehow get better. A related tendency is to deny you had any part in causing the problems in your previous marriage, and then blame all past difficulties on your ex partner.
2. **The second stage is bargaining.** In bargaining, you try anything to repair the damage. You bargain for resolution, usually to no avail. Whether you bargain with God, yourself, an ex-spouse, or even with a new partner, the hallmark of this stage is "magical thinking."
3. **The third stage is anger.** During this time you will be furious at the person who has broken your heart. When one partner in a relationship dies, the other will become angry, decrying how a beloved could have left his partner behind—however illogical this anger may be. It isn't logical, but it is emotionally real. When a marriage dies, it is natural to feel anger about all that you've lost: the effort and dreams, perhaps your money, a house, and other

material assets, or the in-tact home you always wanted for your children. Even though you are at least part of the cause of the result, your anger may be directed at everyone but yourself.

4. **The fourth stage is despair.** When the reality of your loss sets in, depression often takes over. This stage often lasts for some time, and it is important that you tend to your depression lest it grow and become unmanageable. The other pitfall of this stage of grief for the recently divorced is the rush to fall in love, akin to being rescued from a deep moat full of dangerous alligators. Except that the alligators are your own negative feelings, and they must be felt before you are ready for another relationship.

5. **The last stage is acceptance.** You accept your role in the loss of the marriage, although you may still be exploring your own negative behaviors and how you can change them in the future. The key is to see them. In this stage you also accept your ex's part in it, and as much as possible, forgive her.

Each stage in the grieving process is easier to deal with when you understand what is happening and how it fits into the overall process of healing from loss. Only after going through all five stages of grief is your healing complete. Only when you have let the pain out of your heart are you ready for something or something new.

Considering Remarriage

Being single is a time to assess who you are and what you need before you enter your next intimate relationship. Being single is a good time to learn from your past relationships. Rather than becoming upset with your past behaviors, you can listen to and learn from them. For example, stress in a relationship is always a signal that something is wrong. It's important to look at the stress and come to understand it, rather than just accept it or be angry at it. Like the feeling of pain when you touch a hot stove, stress may be telling you that the type of relationship you were in, or are now entering, is inappropriate for you. Once you understand yourself you can guide yourself into a relationship that is more appropriate. Most people have to go through at least one inappropriate relationship in order to create an appropriate one.

In other words, most have to learn from their relationship failures. If this is true, your failures are not really complete failures; rather, they are opportunities to learn more about who you are and what you need in the future to be truly happy. That is the work single people need to do after they have ended an unhappy marriage. Rather than spending valuable time bemoaning the failure or blaming your ex, you can assess what went wrong and what you can change so that your next relationship will be successful. Better to learn and create new mistakes.

 ## Question

What is a rebound marriage?
When you fall in love and marry on the rebound, you're using the infatuation of a new romance like a drug to anesthetize the pain you'd rather not feel from your failed marriage. Anyone who remarries less than three years after the breakdown of a marriage risks undermining the new marriage with unresolved issues and feelings from the previous one.

The tendency to unconsciously transfer old hurts, fears, and resentments from one relationship into the next, painting your new partner with the same colors as your last, are real dangers for those entering a second or third marriage. The definition of insanity is repeatedly doing the same thing and expecting a different outcome. To avoid making this mistake in the context of remarriage, you have to get a clear picture of what went wrong in the past, especially your part in it.

How to Use Your Time Between Marriages

This is the time for the hard work of self-growth, so that you might be ready for a new relationship and possible remarriage. It's also a time to refine your ability to read other people, to notice who triggers your core wound, and what sets off the very negative behaviors that got you and your previous marriage in trouble. It's time for a self-inventory.

Here are some questions to ponder, best after you've spent some time alone or after doing some individual therapy. Write down your answers and put them away. Then reread what you wrote and reflect further. Are you being ruthlessly honest with yourself? Revise based on further evidence and analysis. Part of the process may include sharing your answers with a close friend or counselor.

Self-Inventory for Your Time Between Marriages

- Who am I alone?
- What are my best qualities in relationships? What works? (Examples include expressing appreciation, admitting mistakes, offering constructive criticism)
- What are my least healthy behaviors in relationships? What doesn't work? (Examples are being too quick to get angry, inability to express feelings of sadness, excessive drinking or smoking habits, and so on)
- What more do I need to do to resolve old hurts, past marriage?
- Who do I have to forgive and what must I let go of to be ready to be in a relationship?

You may not presently have all the critically important information about yourself and your behaviors to fully answer this list of questions. Some will become clearer with age and maturity. It is doing the work as well as you can right now that matters. Better yet, before or after you make the jump into another marriage, bring out this list of questions and discuss your answers with your new partner.

This is exactly the sort of knowledge you need to have about each other to deepen your marital relationship. It will also help prepare you to take on and resolve the necessary conflicts that occur in any marriage.

Pitfalls of Remarriages

Most would agree, it is better to be forewarned than to face another divorce. That is why this section examines several common pitfalls affecting second (or third, or fourth) marriages. These factors can plague even those who thought they'd mastered the issues involved, and were aware of the possibility of their rude arrival to disrupt the marriage. These issues can be handled if you openly acknowledge what's not working and try different approaches until you find one that works. Here are some of the common pitfalls of remarriage:

- Unrealistic expectations (for example, that your "prince" will make everything all right)
- Children taking over the marriage relationship, especially in blended families
- The reappearance of the same negative dynamics that dogged previous marriages
- Former spouses who linger and make demands, crowding your new marriage
- Toxic (ex) in-laws who indulge in a blame game left over from a former marriage
- Inability to invest emotionally in new marital relationship because you're still holding on to the last marriage

Each of these pitfalls relates to the basic problems that impact every marriage—sex, children, money, and self—but with the added complexities remarriage brings. There is by definition more emotional baggage in each new remarriage, and the very real fear that you and your partner might repeat the past and face another divorce.

How to View a Prenuptial Agreement

For people over forty, and those individuals or couples with children, personal assets, or inheritances, a prenuptial agreement is a wise and increasingly common aid for sorting out money in a remarriage. Its main purpose is to avoiding financial disputes in the case of either partner's death or a divorce. The prenuptial agreement is especially important when the two come to the marriage with unequal assets, or when one has substantial personal debts or other financial obligations.

It takes two wise people to come to terms with the need for a prenuptial agreement in marriage or remarriage without seeing it as a damper on their new love or a lack of marital trust. Naturally, most often the partner with the most money coming into the marriage is the one who initiates this legal route. In reality, a prenuptial can serve to protect both partners from the strife, pain, and confusion that often accompany the severing of assets when a marriage ends due to death or dissolution. One important issue it covers is the financial protection of children from a previous marriage. The process of coming up with a prenuptial can also serve as a way to focus two people on the need to sort out their money issues before finances become a problem in the relationship.

E ssential

Because you've done this before, you know how hard it is to unmarry. One legal mechanism often put in prenuptial agreements grants different allocations of assets upon death or divorce depending on the length of the marital relationship. Be smart and, if it makes sense for you and your partner, go slowly when merging marital assets.

As discussed in Chapters 6 and 7, marital fights that ostensibly concern money are often about other, deeper issues. Money has a way of revealing a person's core wound, whether she is aware of this old hurt or not. A woman who is perfectly able to earn money may suddenly speak to her husband as if she is a helpless girl speaking to a withholding father. A man who has made a commitment to share his assets with his wife may all of a sudden speak in the resentful tone of a boy in a standoff with his nagging mother. If either or both people would rather not look at these wounds, they may attempt to also avoid the money issues that relate directly to unresolved parent-child emotions. Unfortunately, these issues, overt and covert, tend to come tumbling out at the most inconvenient times: when money is short, when the two of you sit down to sign a mortgage, or when the marriage is already in real trouble. A prenuptial agreement, discussed and negotiated well in advance of the wedding date, is one way to deal with the money issues that if left unresolved can return to haunt your second or third marriage.

Doing Things Differently

People often wonder and ask why the divorce rate is higher for second and third marriages when compared to first marriages. There is an assumption that because people have been through the pain of a marital break-up once, they should have an incentive not to repeat it. They should, after learning from previous mistakes, also (theoretically) possess more relationship skills. Yes, they should have both greater incentive, and better skills, and yet they don't necessarily have either. Call it human nature, but, unfortunately, once you've broken a vow, it's much easier to break the same promise a second time—a reality that contributes to the higher failure rates of each subsequent marriage after your first divorce. Therefore, if you haven't yet filled in the blanks on your self-inventory, now is the time to do so. You stand to grow as an individual, and you may indeed find the right partner for you and with that person cocreate a beautiful and peaceful new relationship.

Chapter 20

A Long-Term Marriage

A LONG-TERM MARRIAGE is usually defined as one lasting two decades or more. Making such a marriage work requires all the skills and understanding covered in this book, plus extraordinary perseverance and a dash of good luck. Fewer than 30 percent of American marriages last this long. Given the many emotional, financial, and spiritual rewards of staying with a partner for two or more decades, it's well worth taking a closer look at the challenges she faces and the keys to her marital success in the long term.

Why Some Marriages Last

For half of first marriages, and 60 percent of second marriages, the emotional trauma often connected with marital failure, the unmet needs of the children, and the negative financial consequences of divorce are insufficient reasons to keep an unhappy husband and wife together when one decides to bolt. Chapter 2 describes the chief reason given for dissolving a marriage as an intolerable level of emotional alienation between spouses. If the failure to meet your partner's emotional needs can destroy a marriage, what does the research have to say about how spouses go about securing a successful long-term marriage?

In their book, *The Second Half of Marriage*, couples workshop leaders David and Claudia Arps report the fascinating results of a written survey they conducted with 500 married men and women about what makes a marriage work beyond the critical seven-year mark. Among all age groups, the factor given as having the greatest impact on continuing marital success was companionship. The majority of respondents (ages thirty to seventy) also put "commitment" to the relationship, "love," and "communication" in the top five of the eight most highly ranked aspects of a positive relationship.

Essential

Many more women are initiating divorces today than men, with most estimates putting the number of female-initiated divorces at two-thirds.

When asked to define those areas that contributed most frequently to marital difficulties, all age groups were again unanimous in listing "financial difficulties" first, while most age groups surveyed put sex as the second most challenging area of marriage. Only those respondents between forty and forty-nine said sex was a highly positive factor contributing to marital success, and no age group gave "romance" a higher number than ten.

All the research on long-term marriage demonstrates an essential truth: marriage requires the nurturing by both partners of a committed, loving friendship. Both of you must also use positive communication to resolve conflicts as you strive to remain each other's closest companion. Beyond these important, general truths, there are many specific challenges you can expect to greet you as your marriage moves past its twentieth anniversary. Fortunately, there are also some time-tested approaches and solutions that can help you and your partner successfully meet every married couple's desire to grow old together.

The Challenges of Long-Term Marriage

After two decades, the marriage has changed drastically and so have you and your partner. These two facts often go unnoticed in today's marriage discussion, despite the fact that so few succeed at marriage over the long haul. Part of what's missing is an understanding of the natural life cycle of a marriage and the stress points that can be expected when individual change conflicts with the changing needs of the partnership.

 Fact

> According to the U.S. Census Bureau, in 1996, the last year data were collected, 52 percent of married couples had been married for at least fifteen years, 20 percent had passed their thirty-fifth anniversary, and 5 percent had been together for fifty years or more.

As a result of their survey and work with couples, David and Claudia Arp concluded that the top challenges in a long-term marriage include:

- Letting go of past marital disappointments
- Shifting back from a child focus to a partner focus
- Maintaining good communication
- Mastering conflict constructively
- Becoming better friends
- Renewing romance and sexuality
- Redefining your goals for the marriage

Each of these challenges requires you make conscious and positive responses to those natural changes that are part of the cycles of a typical long-term marriage.

If Yours Is an Empty Nest

You and your partner have just deposited your last adult child and a small truckload of his belongings at a dormitory, gave the new freshman a long hug (away from his roommates), and now find yourselves in the car driving home—but after a rush of relief you don't know what to make of the knot in your stomach that just appears to be getting tighter by the minute (and mile), your head lighter. What's going on? For one thing, part of you is aware that you and your husband are about to start a brand new chapter of your marriage full of unknowns, with many possible joys and perils.

If you're like many midlife parents who, for the first time in eighteen or more years, are without children in the house, there are major adjustments to be made. No more demands or noise of the children to bother you or buffer your marital relationship. No more complicated adolescent moods to untangle—just your own complex feelings, perhaps a mix of jubilation and fear. Instead of stolen moments, you have limitless privacy. But what will you do with it? In a word, reconnect.

After sharing with your partner a well-deserved pat on the back (for your Herculean roles in successfully getting a child out of the house and onto the next phase of life), it's time to refocus your attention on the next phase of your marriage relationship. Although much attention—and undue pressure—may be put on recharging your sex life at this transition, it's far better to begin any attempt at a marital renaissance with a decision to nurture your emotional intimacy, which very often has also been stretched and neglected as you've navigated the end of adolescence, college applications, tuition, and the final sendoff of this child.

Your empty nest is both a reality and a symbol. Perhaps there's more physical room for one of you to set up a home office, take on a hobby, or create a nice guest room to have old friends come for extended visits, but beware filling this space too soon. It's easy to become distracted from the harder and perhaps long-avoided need to retrace where your emotional connection may have gotten frayed or snapped, to repair the fabric of your marriage.

Marriage Changes You, Too

If it's been a long time since you've taken stock of your marital relationship, be brave but also be gentle when you begin the process. Resist the urge to look only at your partner's perceived deficiencies. In other words, don't project your fears or feelings onto him. "He says the same things over and over" is not a constructive beginning. Instead, start by looking at yourself. If you find your conversations becoming repetitive, ask yourself, are you secretly afraid that you've become predictable and boring? Then go further and search for parts of you that may be stuck, where you're afraid to allow change or growth to occur.

One of the most important blessings of long-term marriage is the opportunity it affords two people to assist each other in making personal and spiritual growth. It can also provide a buffer between you and the outside world that inhibits this sort of individual evolution. With the demands of children and managing a household it's easy to rationalize maintaining the status quo of a relationship that may have long ago become stagnant—meaning the marriage remains safe but not exciting or challenging to either of you.

This stasis can last as long as the two partners remain complicit in keeping it so, or until one "falls in love" with someone else, or a loss befalls one or both of you in the form of illness or the death of a child or another loved one. Or, if you're lucky, your "wake-up call" comes in the form of a more gentle push, such as the departure of the last child from the family home or a retirement, or better yet, the inspiration of one of you to make a change.

The Midlife Married Woman

As a woman makes the transition from her forties into the fifties, she makes a biological shift into menopause, a change often accompanied by a major psychological transformation. If she lived most of her life as a people-pleaser, focused on her relationships, she may get caught up in a new interest, or find a cause to make all her own. For some women, this is the time to focus 100 percent on career goals, or start a small business. As Gail Sheehy puts it, a midlife woman enters her "feisty fifties," and then her "selective sixties," both reflecting a shift from being other focused to a new emphasis on self-mastery.

The Midlife Married Man

Again, according to Gail Sheehy and other researchers, the midlife man also undergoes major physical and psychological transformations. With the drop in his testosterone level, a fifty-something male wants and needs sex less often. Many men report finding this shift a relief from the constant urge to be sexual, an opportunity to invest emotionally in relationships and other interests. To many female partners of men going through this change of life, these are welcome shifts.

However, it's also true that while many fifty-something women are revving up for a new more ambitious stage of life and work, their male partners are in a downshifting mode, anticipating time off, travel, and more attention from their partners. For the long-time married couple these are significant individual changes that can have a huge impact on your relationship.

 Question

Are midlife women less interested in sex?
No, not necessarily. Counter to this widespread myth, a 1999 survey of women of different age groups found that of the 31 percent of women who reported low sexual desire, 64 percent were under the age of thirty-nine. Among women in their fifties, the number who reported a low sexual desire dropped to 27 percent.

Examining the Long-Term Marriage

When it comes time to review the strengths and weaknesses in your marriage, The Marriage Self-Test (Appendix A) may be a useful tool to use to jump-start the process. As you assess your marital communication, ask yourself whether sex with your partner is meeting your needs, and ponder if you are still stronger and better as a couple than you would be as an individual. You must also find out whether both or one of you is interested in improving the marriage. It's an important time of transition, but if only one of you is willing and ready deal with the need for a change in the status quo, it can be an even more delicate and challenging time. As discussed in Chapter 15, one partner's emotional growth can sometimes be enough to change a marriage for the better. It also may lead to that partner's restructuring of the marriage. For example, you may make a decision to spend more time apart pursuing independent interests, which enables the relationship to continue while making room for internal changes.

Ideally, both of you wish to invest new energy in your long-term marriage, with the twin goals of ensuring its duration and quality. If you've taken the Marriage Self-Test, you can use the data you've collected to draw up a set of new emotional and practical objectives for the relationship—not unlike those you drew up in Chapter 3 (to structure a working partnership) and Chapter 7 (to compare money values and plan the next decades of your lives)—together.

Essential

Forgiveness means forgiving yourself for the dreams you have not managed to fulfill, both within your marriage and alone. This is an essential step before you can let go of those dreams, along with any resentment you may be holding toward your partner for her possible role in bringing about your disappointments.

Here are some questions about the current state and future of your marriage for the two of you to answer—as a team:

- **Examine the strengths of your marriage.** How much do you enjoy each other's company and/or share common interests?
- **Next, take an honest look at its weaknesses.** It may be that you don't make time to enjoy the things you're both interested

in. Or, you have stopped expressing affection, leaving one or both of you feeling lonely or unloved.

- **Name your top three goals for the marriage.** You want to travel together. You want to revitalize your sex. You want to work another ten years and save as much as possible for retirement. You want to make room for each of you to do things apart that both have been yearning to try. You want to take a walk together every morning.

If you treat this process seriously, tackling differences and affirming similarities, you'll end up with a working agreement that can guide you through the next phase of marriage.

Moving Beyond the Tried and True

Couples at any point can face feelings of boredom, or relationship doldrums—that sense that the two of you have the same conversations over and over and have nothing new to talk about. Yet, there are couples who never run out of things to say to each other. What these couples often share is a burning curiosity, not just about each other but also the world around them. One source of this curiosity and sense of aliveness is one's desire for self-knowledge and self-growth, as well as the potential for growth in relationship to his partner.

There are many ways to foster this quality in your long-term marriage. How often do you suggest a new topic of conversation with your partner? Do you ever invite him to join you on a trip to a museum, or try a new sport or activity; how about golf, bridge, or poker? This is also a great time to consider taking a couples' workshop together. In a group therapeutic process you can receive support by watching other couples go through similar struggles and receive feedback and guidance on your own.

The Marriage Renewal Ceremony

Many couples, upon reaching their silver or any other meaningful anniversary, use this occasion to mark a milestone and plan for the future. After reviewing and releasing the past, and drawing up an agreement for the next phase of marriage, they choose to memorialize these actions with a marriage renewal ceremony.

If you would like to incorporate this ritual into your marriage, you can invite family and friends and recite your vows in front of them, just as you did for your original wedding. You may also choose to hold a celebratory reception. Like a marriage, or the christening of a newborn child, the purpose of such a ceremony is twofold: to assist the couple to take in the importance of the passage they've marked, and to ask for and receive the recognition and support of the larger community for their renewed marriage.

Planning for the Future

Whether yours is a newer marriage of two people at midlife or a long-term marriage in which you're approaching midlife, you must face the certainty that old age awaits you and that one of you will outlive the other. If you are like the typical couple in the Arps's survey of the long-term married cited earlier, joint financial management was likely to have been a challenging area for the two of you, too. Now, however, mastering it, or obtaining professional help to handle financial planning, is of critical importance. All sources of joint and individual assets and income—real estate, pensions, investments, estimated Social Security payments due to you—as well as liabilities, including any mortgages or other debts, must be assessed carefully.

No one knows how long he'll live, or whether he'll outlive his partner. But this is the time when you can give each other the great gift of peace of mind by making concrete one of the key agreements of marriage: to see to each other's welfare in sickness and health. And, to carry out the wish of most married couples, to help the one left behind in whatever material ways you can by careful planning.

Health Concerns
In addition to maintaining health insurance until age sixty-five, and eventually availing oneself of Medicare, the choice of whether to purchase long-term-care insurance must be considered by each

person independently and each couple together, and, with the complexities involved, many benefit by consulting with an insurance professional as early in midlife as possible. For one thing, the younger you are when you enlist in such coverage, the lower the monthly premiums are likely to be. On the other side, the net cost of these earlier payments may outweigh any potential savings. A rule of thumb used by many financial advisors is if you have more than $50,000 in liquid assets, long-term-care insurance can be an important way to preserve wealth.

Housing Concerns

The main choice faced by midlife couples, especially empty nesters, is whether to downsize from the family home to a home built for two. Into this decision-making process should go any knowledge you have at midlife about health issues, such as a bad back or arthritis, conditions that should inform choices such as stairs, counter heights, and locations of rooms. It's also valuable to begin acquiring a knowledge of senior housing options including active retirement communities, planned senior housing, and assisted living—all common options for couples beginning as early as age fifty-five.

 Question

Why is turbulence in a long-term marriage healthy?
A marriage that works is able to withstand conflict, and it can accommodate the airing of strong differences without falling apart under the stress. The commitment is strong enough to withstand temporary discomfort, and the couple has learned that anxiety or pain can also lead to growth and positive change.

Joys of Long-Term Marriage

If you've managed to stay married past the twenty-year mark or beyond, you are entitled to feel great pride in this accomplishment. You stuck it out when things got tough. You've forgiven innumerable slights, even a partner's grave trespasses. In short, you've learned how to roll with all the good and bad that a long-term marriage can serve up.

Becoming Grandparents, Together

One of the near-universally adored experiences in life is being a grandparent. Although with today's blended families, you have as much chance of becoming a step-grandparent as a biological one, if you have the exquisite pleasure of sharing this experience in a long-term marriage with a biological grandchild, the two of you have taken the grand prize. The precise nature of this relationship depends of course on geographic distance and the wishes of the child's parents. The other caution is treating the shaping of this grandparent-grandchild relationship as a joint decision with your spouse, not making it an either/or proposition.

Companions for Life

At each stage of marriage, the constant factor determining the quality of your lives together is the friendship that forms the foundation of your relationship. In a long-term marriage, you've been with your best friend for a quarter, perhaps a third or more of your lives. Nothing can replace the trust and intimacy of such a long and rich friendship. Without a doubt, the secret of maintaining this friendship within marriage for as long as you have is your combined ability to be open to change and personal growth.

It's equally important to recognize that keeping a marriage fresh is hard work. In their book, *The Best Half of Life*, Ray and Anne Ortlund make this point eloquently when they write, "We don't naturally drift closer together, we drift further apart. We have to fight our way back to each other, day after day, year after year, as long as we live." So what does a true marriage of loving companions look and sound like? It's looking up from a book or greeting a spouse at the end of the day with the simple thought, "I'm so glad you're here." And then, beginning your first sentence with the words, "I just can't wait to tell you. . . ." These are the priceless joys of long-term marriage.

Appendix A

The Marriage Self-Test

HOW WOULD YOU rate the quality of your relationship? If you are like most married people you have both good and challenging times in your marriage. The problem is that most live in this constant see-saw state and never really examine where the relationship is strong and where it is weak. Is there a way to measure or quantify your relationship so you can know and communicate where the challenges are, where you are succeeding, and how serious the problems may be? The purpose of this Marriage Self-Test is to help you do just that.

Why Grade Your Marriage?

The purpose of this scale is to assist you in measuring the quality of your relationship. You may wonder if you can answer questions about how you feel about your relationship that would tell you and your partner (and possibly your therapist) where the problems are and how serious the problems may be. The answer is yes. Of course, such a scale would be very subjective as it is based completely upon your feelings about your relationship.

Since feelings are irrational and will fluctuate according to your mood and circumstance, this limits the degree of scientific accuracy of such a test. However, you will still find it worthwhile to answer these basic questions, and then, after grading your answers, compare your reactions and feelings with your partner.

If you find you agree on areas that are weak, then you have a good place to begin working on the issues in your marriage. Some of your answers may surprise your partner, and this would be another good place to begin talking about why you answered the question as you did.

Using the Grading Scale

Answer the following ten questions rating your answer to each question by placing it in one of five categories. These five categories are very good, good, acceptable, fair, and poor. Then assign the appropriate number to each answer: Very good = 5, good = 4, acceptable = 3, fair = 2, and poor = 1. Once you complete the ten questions, you must add the numbers to get a score that can be used to help evaluate the relationship. Most working relationships should have a score around 30. If you find that your score falls below that number, you might want to find ways to improve the areas that drag down the score. Above 30 you are blessed with a good relationship.

The Test Questions

To begin, answer the following questions strictly from your own viewpoint. Do not ask your partner what he feels the answer should be. For example, question number ten asks, "How do you rate your communication skills within this relationship?" What you're asked to assess in this question is whether, strictly from your own point of view, you (not the two of you) have good communications skills as manifested in the communications that occur between you and your partner. He too should answer this and the other nine questions strictly from *his* perspective. Once you each complete the test, compare answers and find out where you are weak and where you are strong.

1. How would you rate the overall satisfaction level you feel about your relationship?

Poor   fair   acceptable   good   very good

2. How would you rate your partner's feelings of overall satisfaction?

Poor   fair   acceptable   good   very good

3. Do you trust your partner?

Poor   fair   acceptable   good   very good

4. Are you able to be completely honest with your partner?

Poor   fair   acceptable   good   very good

5. Do you feel free to express yourself as an individual without losing your feeling of also being a couple?

Poor   fair   acceptable   good   very good

6. Are you able to find contented consensus when you want different outcomes?

Poor   fair   acceptable   good   very good

7. Do you feel a deep commitment to your relationship?

Poor   fair   acceptable   good   very good

8. Do you respect your partner?

Poor   fair   acceptable   good   very good

9. Are you sexually attracted to your partner? Is there magic in the relationship?

Poor   fair   acceptable   good   very good

10. How do you rate your communication skills within this relationship?

Poor   fair   acceptable   good   very good

Appendix B

Resources: Recommended Books and Websites

Books

Gottman, John M., and Nan Silver. *The Seven Principles for Making Marriage Work* (New York: Three Rivers Press, 1999).

Hendricks, Gay, and Kathyln Hendricks. *Conscious Loving: The Journey to Co-Commitment* (New York: Bantam, 1992).

Hendrix, PhD, Harville. *Getting the Love You Want* (New York: Henry Holt, 1988).

Johnson, Robert A. *We: Understanding the Psychology of Romantic Love* (San Francisco: Harper & Row, 1983).

Mosely, Doug, and Naomi Mosely. *Making Your Second Marriage a First Class Success* (Rocklin, CA: Prima, 1998).

Wallerstein, Judith S. *The Unexpected Legacy of Divorce* (New York: Hyperion, 2000).

Wellwood, John. *Challenge of the Heart* (Boston: Shambala, 1985).

Websites

www.healmarriage.com

Stephen Martin's website contains articles on marriage and family relationships, contact information, and a schedule for his Making Marriage Work couples' workshops.

www.ivillage.com

"When you say I do" love and marriage-related articles and community: forums, columns, and resources with an emphasis on needs and interests of younger women.

www.thirdage.com/relationships-sex

A community website for forty-plus men and women: articles, columns, and forums on long-term marriage and midlife marriages.

Index

P

Parenting, 167–79, 190. *See also* Children; Stepfamilies
Partners before parents, 168–69
Partnership, 37–38. *See also* Teamwork

Passion, 123–36. *See also* Sex
reawakening, 129–30
rekindling, 127–29
and sexuality, 123–36
Past events, 24, 183–84, 253–54
Physical abuse, 242–43
Picking fights, 53–57. *See also* Fair fighting rules
"Pin money," 103–4
"Plan B," 14–15
Platonic love, 25
Poetry, 119
Power play, 63, 160
Power sharing, 31–42
Practice and teamwork, 4–7
Pregnancy, 120–22
Premarital counseling, 4, 219, 227–28
Prenuptial agreements, 260–61
Private issues, 8–9, 63
Problem child, 176. *See also* Children
Professional help, 173–76. *See also* Marriage therapy
Projections, 9

R

Rebound marriage, 257
Reconcilable differences, 155–57
Religious differences, 231–32
Remarriage, 253–61
and broken hearts, 254–56
considering, 256–57
and divorce rates, 261
and in-laws, 259
learning from past, 253–54

pitfalls of, 259
prenuptial agreements, 260–61
on the rebound, 257
and self-assessment, 258–59
Resources, 279–80
Respect within family, 170–73
Role-playing, 132–35
Romance, 117–20
Romantic love, xv, 3, 118–20, 154, 220. *See also* Love
Rules of fair fighting, 61–81

S

The Second Half of Marriage, 264
Self, 153–65
and boundaries, 154, 157–58, 162
and control, 159–62
and differences, 155–57
not losing, 153–55
and partner's needs, 6
and separateness, 163–65
and togetherness, 163–65
and unconditional love, 158–59
understanding, xv, 15
Self-assessment, 258–59, 267
Self-test, 16, 268–69, 275–78
Separateness, 26–27, 147, 163–65, 224–25
Separations, 248–49. *See also* Divorce
Sex, 111–22
by appointment, 120
communicating about, 112–17, 127–28
deepening connections, 15, 122–25
experiences with, 126–27
fantasy games, 132–35
frequency of, 22–23, 114
fresh starts, 129–30
importance of, 21–23
and intimacy, 111–13
and newlyweds, 220–21